A striking reminder that adversity can refine us, not define us. Dr. Robison's story offers strength to anyone navigating a tough season.
Aaron Poynton | Author, Bestselling Author, *Think Like A Black Sheep*

The emotional depth of these pages took me by surprise. Dr. Robison shows how faith can carry you through storms you never saw coming.
Aslak de Silva | USA National Bestselling Author

Show Them takes a thoughtful, integrated look at healing that considers the full scope of the human experience without over-simplifying it. Dr. Robison approaches a complex subject with clarity and care, offering a perspective that invites reflection rather than easy answers.
Brandon Blewett | Author, *How to Avoid Strangers on Airplanes*

Dr. Robison writes with the authority of a physician and the humility of someone who has been tested again and again. His lessons are real, raw, and transformational.
Casel Burnett | Vice President, LODI, and International Bestselling Author of *No Regrets*

His courage to step into the unknown inspired me to reflect on my own path. Each challenge he faced became a source of growth and compassion, and that unwavering spirit is what makes this book truly shine.
Glenn Hopper | Author, *AI Mastery for Finance Professionals*

This book is a beautiful blend of grit, gratitude, and grace. Dr. Robison doesn't just tell his story; he shares the tools that helped him rise.
Tamara Nall | CEO & Founder, The Leading Niche

Dr. Glen N. Robison's Show Them is a powerful testament to faith, persistence, and keeping promises to God. From battling severe asthma and academic rejection to becoming a surgeon and serving in Tonga, Glen shows that 'No means Go' when rooted in trust in God's plan. His honest stories of trials, near-death moments, and Abrahamic tests will inspire believers to see hardship as preparation for greater purpose. This memoir reminds us God can turn the odds in our favor. Highly recommended.
Carl Grant III | Author, *How to Live the Abundant Life*

From dyslexia to life-or-death moments, he somehow turns every setback into a stepping stone. It's hard not to feel empowered after reading his journey.
Trissa Tismal-Capili | USA Today and Wall Street Journal Bestselling Author

As a previously struggling entrepreneur who lived like Dr. Robison, the Horatio Alger lifestyle story, Dr. Robison's book is the embodiment of living through trial and tribulations. Determined, you will survive and thrive yourself into becoming a fulfilled and successful human being. My congratulations to Dr. Robison on a wonderful and inspiring literary piece of work.
Darius Ross | Managing Director, D Alexander Ross Real Estate Capital Partners Interest LLC

SHOW THEM

Stepping Into the Unknown to Find the Answers

DR GLEN N ROBISON

ISBN **979-8-99347-610-0** (pbk)
ISBN **979-8-99347-611-7** (hcv)
ISBN **979-8-99347-612-4** (ebook)

Library of Congress Control Number: **2025922569**

Table of Contents

Introduction

Lying on a hard gurney in the X-ray room, the needle broke through the surface of my left arm, while small drops of blood splattered onto the floor like raindrops falling from the sky. The last of the contrast dye fluid was pushed into my arm; CODE BLUE CODE BLUE blasted from the hospital's loudspeaker. Multiple medical staff frantically rushed in to see who was blue in the room; unfortunately, it was me. Waiting for the doctor to arrive to give the orders on what lifesaving medications to give, I took my last normal breath of life. What felt like minutes was a four-hour ordeal of the rapid response team trying to resuscitate me. They were doing everything physically below to get me to breathe while I was taken into the most peaceful place that I have ever traveled to from above, then suddenly, I joined in and helped them bring me back to life. How did I help? It was a thought in spirit form that allowed me to ask if I could come back to honor a once-in-a-life-time promise that I had made to my brother.

As each page unfolds, you will read over 150 personal stories of my life from the time I discovered I loved medicine, to the time I was staring at a live beating heart in a chest cavity in my surgical residency. What makes my life interesting is that I was told that I would never make it into college by my high school counselor. I will also take you on a journey that has many ups and downs, laughs and tears, disappointments, and accomplishments. I will share with you the time in my life when life came to a screech-ing halt. It pushed me to make a decision as to whether I should continue breathing or end it and go to the place where I once experienced total peace. I will share with you my life, death, and overcoming the odds on this million-mile journey.

Here is a small glimpse of a few more stories you will experience, along with some valuable teaching principles that have been my benchmark for life.

Story #1: When the Odds Were Against Me at a Very Young Age, I Had to *Show Them*

Grabbing my rubber basketball and racing out the door, I yelled for my dog, Bear, to come. She was always excited to run along with me on the dirt roads in the hills just above town where I lived. While Bear was so preoccupied with chasing rabbits and other critters, I was strategically dribbling in between the potholes to pretend they were my defenders and trying to steal the ball away from me. Occasionally, the ball would hit a rock, and I would have to run after it. I did my best to maneuver around the potholes, dribbling with my right hand and then my left hand. It was my goal to make the basketball team and eventually go on to college and even pursue it professionally, but deep down, my goal was to find a cure for my breathing difficulties, and I used basketball as my motivation.

I just wanted to be normal like all the other kids as they ran with no breathing difficulties. Each day I ran, I kept a record of when my asthma attack started, what I did, and whether I ran further than the day before the attack happened. What other factors played into this? What did I eat that day that may have caused the asthma attack sooner, which led me to pay closer attention to what I ate? That young, curious mind of mine fueled my aspiration and revealed the roots of resilience that would carry me forward.

Story #2: The Power of a Promise

Do we truly understand the power of our words when we make a promise to a friend, a family member, or even a stranger?

When I was in college, my best friend, who was born in Tonga, helped me through some classes that I had difficulty with. I remember the day, while walking through the hallways in the library, I said to him, "If I ever make it through medical school, I will go to Tonga and treat your people." Eleven years later, I was boarding a plane that took me to this remote island in the South

Pacific. Little did I know this simple promise ended up affecting so many people.

The power of a promise! Even if it took eleven years to fulfill, across distance and time, a crisis becomes a catalyst for action and a vocation to serve.

Deep in the South Pacific, on a remote Island of Nuku'alofa, a young boy was so excited to play with his cousin and friends on his birthday. As the cousin was the first to show up, the two of them began to play in the yard.

Their excitement took them into the front yard and too close to the roadway. Not aware of the oncoming traffic, one of those cars came around the corner and missed the cousin but hit the birthday boy, dragging him down the gravel driveway. In the meantime, the parents were making final preparations for the big party, and they heard screams from their boy and his cousin, as they rushed to the sounds of the screams, only to see their child underneath the car. Finding what they could to wrap the child's leg that was shredded by the gravel with flesh dangling off and blood spurting everywhere, they applied pressure to the leg and rushed him to the hospital.

Leaving the child in the hands of the medical staff, trusting they would hold their child again, they said their silent prayers and put their trust in God. The nurses went right to work to control the bleeding and then bandaged the leg, and waited for the doctor to show up on Monday, when he was due to come back in.

Little did I know that I would be a part of the medical team making a decision that would save this boy's life and leg. Did this child ever walk again? Join me on my journey to find out.

You will also find each moment throughout the book. Here are three examples you, the reader, can gain and hopefully implement into your life.

Teaching Moment #1: Patiently Believing + Persistence Equals Success. What Persistence Did I Have to Endure? I Had to *Show Them*, Even Though It Took Many Years

The path through medical training and personal hardship unfolds, shaping who I am becoming. I will also share with you what it was like to be the only student in my medical class who never received a bachelor's degree, and what it was like to have failed the National Board's Part I four times but pass it on the final attempt. What was it like sleeping at a bus stop, trying to find a place to live my first semester in medical school, and still trying to keep up with my studies? One of the hardest things I had to do was not compare myself to the other students who excelled academically. I knew if I could make it to the clinicals, I could have more hands-on experience, and I could **Show Them** my true skills.

Teaching Moment #2: What to Do When You Are in Your Own Personal Abrahamic Moment

A new term, a new lens—the Abrahamic moment—frames the turning point toward purpose and renewal. What is an Abrahamic moment? It is an event that pushes you beyond your limits; it is the point at which the inner pressure causes you to ask: Is it worth it to persist, or do I end it because I can't handle it anymore? In simple terms, it is the ultimate frustrations of life that are out of your control. It is different than depression because if you step out of the situation that makes you frustrated, and you become the observer and not the participant, unexplained opportunities start to happen for your own good. My very personal chapter opens—fatherhood, family, and the test that changed everything.

Teaching Moment #3: Why Do We Put Limits on Ourselves? "No Means Go"

Every great thing in life started with a thought, and every thought that led to greatness started with a question. Is there one question that you have never answered? For myself, it was "Who am I?" When I was swimming around in my mom's tummy, waiting to come out screaming, I must have asked, "How in the world am I going to get out of here?" While everyone else in the outside world was asking if it was a boy or a girl as they rubbed my mom's tummy. Life cannot exist without a question, even though this book started with a question. The questions that followed shaped my path, and the path itself became my teacher of life, or what I would say, "experiences are your greatest teacher."

In my journey, I have been associated with many titles (Surgical Resident, Student, Coach, Doctor, Physician, Surgeon, Myopractor, Practitioner, Artist, Author, Husband, and Father). There was not a single title, as just mentioned, that did not have some form of challenges, heartache, trials, discouragements, and achievements. My motivating factor was triggered by someone telling me I couldn't do it. All it took was the word NO that set the course for the rest of my journey. To me, "No means Go." From doubt to action, the next pages trace how a single phrase became a compass.

Stepping Into the Unknown to Find the Answers

The subtitle invites you into the unknown with courage, for the answers you seek are not found in the safety of the shore, but in the faithful movement of taking that first brave step. It won't always be easy, but I promise you that the version of yourself waiting on the other side of the mystery is worth every bit of the climb.

I am often asked how I find time to write, paint, be a doctor, and a surgeon. I replied, "I don't have to find the time, time finds me!" Why put limits on yourself? Who says you can only do one thing? The key thing is to focus on what is in front of you. I had many experiences that became the greatest teachers in life. Each one will be highlighted to show you a new experience I faced on my million-mile journey through life, death, and overcoming the odds.

Here are my five things that I hope you can gain from my life experiences.

1. Use the word "**NO**" to your advantage and make it your springboard to fulfilling your dreams and desires. Use the word "**NO**" and combine it with **Faith** to see that all things are possible.
2. **When everything is against you**, it's only a matter of time before the opposing forces show you that **everything will be for you**. Trust the process, stay patient, and be persistent in the process.
3. Your **True Potential** is often only seen at the last breath of life. Could the lights be your true potential? Don't wait for it; do something today to see it.
4. **Promises** are more than just words; they are powerful text messages sent out into the universe to start the unimaginable events that happen in the future.
5. At some point, every one of us will go through an "**Abrahamic Moment**" event that pushes us to the very edge of our questions. Mine happened to be not seeing my children after my divorce; just know the night is darkest right before the lights of the morning horizon. Choose to see your trial as a teaching moment, something to learn from, no matter how painful it is. When this happens, your hidden talents and gifts will be beyond your own comprehension. Choose to learn from it and then let go and let God show you your charted course that he is so wanting to show you.

If I have caught your attention, please read on and see the stories unfold, and let the teaching moments propel you to greater heights. Are you ready to take this journey with me?

CHAPTER 1

Breathing Through a Straw

People don't understand that when I grew up, I was never the most talented. I was never the biggest, I was never the fastest, I certainly was never the strongest; the only thing I had was my work ethic, and that's been what has gotten me this far.

– Tiger Woods

If you want to know what it was like for me as a child, pick up a straw, take a breath in, and then exhale your breath through the same straw for about five minutes. Now you get a small glimpse of what it was like to breathe each night and all night. This was my life as a child and even in my college years.

From the feeling of constant breathlessness, let me step back and show you the place and circumstances that surrounded my childhood.

I have a hunch that my early childhood asthma came from multiple things. The house that I lived in was an old gas station my father bought for $2,500 and remodeled it into a two and ¼ bedroom house. One room for the boys, one room for the girls, with basically a closet for my parents. At the beginning of my life, my bedroom was on the kitchen floor until my dad had the time, money, and resources to build another room. As I began to connect my environment with my symptoms, questions started to surface and shape how I understood my asthma.

Gas station turned into the house where I was raised.

Breathing Through a Straw Was Difficult and Exhausting

From my own observation, I asked myself questions that triggered my asthma. I knew my asthma was worse at night and while exercising, but it was also triggered by the cold and at certain times of the year. Was it being picked last in every sport that I wanted to participate in? Or was it because I was the smallest and weakest kid? I just loved sports so much, but sports did not love me back. Why was I the child out of the nine children who had the worst asthma? I was not born with it, nor did I have it until I was about four years old. So, what happened after the age of four when I first started to experience my asthma attacks? Could it have been from the coal-burning stove to heat the house, or from the clothes my father would wear on the farm that would be tossed into the laundry basket outside my bedroom door?

These questions propelled my young mind to find a cure, so I could be normal like all the other boys and girls who ran freely with no breathing difficulties. Each day was like breathing through a straw. I strongly feel the reasons why I had such a difficult time in school were just pure exhaustion from being up all night trying to breathe. I could not fully concentrate on what the teacher was saying, and my comprehension level was below average. Maybe this wanting to find a cure for asthma helped me to prepare for one of the most disappointing announcements in high school when my counselor told me that I would never make it into college. I feel this one event set things into motion to become a surgeon when becoming one was not even on my radar at that time.

The One Dollar per Piano Lesson My Mom Charged Paid for My Doctor Bills

My mom would teach piano lessons for one dollar per hour; she must have taught everyone in my hometown how to play the piano. She used this money to take me to the doctors to see if they had any answers to help me breathe better. We had no health insurance for the family, so going to the doctors was a rarity. She did not want to see me suffer, and so she did what any mother would do when they could not come up with an answer: she resorted to seeking out help. The clinic that my mom took me to recommended allergy shots, and I did this for several years. Then one day, after getting my shot, I was walking to the baseball fields to go to practice. I was only halfway there when suddenly, I fell to the ground, gasping for air. Luckily, I fell right in front of my classmate's house. Did one of my guardian angels inform the person in the house to come out at the time to only to find me on their lawn, grasping for air?

I was taken back to the hospital where the clinic was, and they must have given me something to counteract the reaction. It was later discovered that the allergy shot that I got had expired.

My mom did not have me take any more of these shots and just resorted to the inhaler when the asthma attack happened.

Even as medical attempts came and went, daily life at home kept its rhythm, and so did our routines around the table.

Family Get-Together at the Dinner Table

The one time the family got together was at dinner time, Dad would sit at the head of the table, and I would be sandwiched in between my other brothers on the bench. There was very little talking at the table. In a way, it was a fueling station to recharge, only to go back to either the farm or the family projects outside that needed to be finished before it got too dark to see. Mom would prepare all the breakfasts, lunches, and dinners; she cooked from scratch, with the one exception of *Corn Flakes*, the cheapest store-bought cereal from the store. Now, when you combine that with powdered milk, I would pick the smallest bowl off the shelf, take two big gulps, and then go to school. Most mornings, I would time it just right so I would wake up, put my clothes on, and make sure I had just enough time to get to school, purposely skipping breakfast.

The Time My Mom Said I Was Going to Be a Doctor While on Our Sunday Drive

As a child, I looked forward to the Sunday afternoon family trips in the mountains. My father asked all my brothers and sisters to get in the truck. Most of us joined my mom in the bed of the truck. I enjoyed listening to her stories of when she would visit the ranch with her father.

That day in the back of the truck while my dad drove the family in the mountains, my mom said out of the blue, "Glen is going to be the doctor in the family." Without missing a beat, she went on to tell her story about being raised on a ranch in Arizona. "Why would she say that?" I thought to myself. And how is that even possible? I could barely read or write, let alone spell anything correctly. My teachers would tell me I was stupid and put me in special education classes.

I always pondered what possessed my mom to say that. Was it her observing my excitement when I got a doctor bag for my birthday when I was in kindergarten? Or was it when I ran home after school to tell her about how I dissected a cow heart in class in the 6th grade? Maybe she saw my passion to find a cure for asthma as I ran with Bear (my dog) every evening with a basketball.

All I can tell you is that those words that she spoke that day planted a seed so deep that nothing was going to uproot it, not even a discouraging word or unexpected disappointment. I trusted her words because she never lied to me. Because she said I could do it, nothing else mattered. That seed grew into a promise, and the promise carried through every doubt.

Sunday afternoon trip in the mountains.

My First Business Partner Who Helped Me Buy My First Bike

Here's how that partnership began and the dream that sparked it. One day at school, I noticed a classmate who rode his bike to school. It was the coolest thing ever; it was hot, metallic, fire red, with fiberglass spokes. Seeing that bike caused a burning desire inside me to make money to buy one myself. I discussed my plan with my mom, and she told me that if I can make half of the money to buy the bike, she will help me with the other half. I eagerly started to collect soda pop bottles and took them to the local grocery store to exchange for ten cents a bottle.

I will never forget the day I got my bike; the smell of its fiberglass rims and black tires, and the vibrant metallic fiery ruby red color that put a smile on my face that went from ear to ear.

That first bike opened the door to bigger rides—and to my ongoing quest to understand my asthma.

I eventually upgraded my bike and got a ten-speed and would take that bike on 10-mile rides to the next town, or across the mountains. I used all forms of exercise to help me figure out what was triggering my asthma, and I still resorted to dribbling a basketball in the hills above town as I ran with my dog Bear. It was my goal to perfect my ball-handling skills along with finding the cure for asthma. During all these exercises, I would record how far into the exercise it took to get an asthma attack, and I would also record what foods I ate that may have been the cause. I was on a mission to find a cure for asthma.

Beyond bikes and experiments, my story always circles back to the person at the center of my life—my mom.

Mom: "My Best Friend"

Not only was my mother my first business partner, but she was also more than a mother to me; I just happened to be her constant little shadow. I love spending time with her in the garden planting all the vegetables in perfect rows, and watering them each day to see the little sprouts of the peas, corn, and carrots start to make their way to the blue skies. She was my personal life coach; she never spoke a negative word. I did not need a shot of Red Bull; I just needed her words, like you can do anything you put your mind to, or don't let anyone ruin your day. She was the energy drink that I needed for the day. If we were not in the garden helping the vegetables grow, we would be in the orchard helping the apple, apricot, and pear trees. When she had time, she would walk us to the local park to play. She would point out flowers and trees, and really showed me the beauty of nature. When she was teaching piano lessons, I was there listening to her give instructions to her student. She was my personal angel on earth.

Peach Tree in a Bottle: What Kind of Seed Is This?

One memory in particular captured what it was like hanging out with my mom. The garden wasn't just chores—it was where lessons and stories took root. Working with my mom in the garden was my one-on-one time with her; the other brothers and sisters looked at pulling weeds as physical work, but I, on the other hand, looked at this as a great opportunity to learn something. That's when a tiny discovery became a tradition—and a taste I'll never forget.

One day while working in the garden, I noticed a new little plant poking its small branches out of the soil. I asked my mom if that was a weed and if I should pull it up. She said it was a peach tree. "Do you remember the big seeds we threw by the garden after eating peaches?" she asked. "I do remember," I replied. She said we should find a special place for it so we can water it and attend to it, and maybe one day eat peaches from it.

Over the years, I would do as my mom told me. In the winter months, I would keep it covered and protect it from the deep snowfalls. As I was growing out of my pants, so was my tree; it too was growing taller than me. One day, I got a phone call while playing at my friend's house. It was my mother. She said, "Glen, it is time to come home, your peaches are ready to be picked and bottled." I eagerly ran home, grabbed my buckets from the shed, and she showed me which peaches to pick and which ones to leave on the tree. She then helped me take the buckets of peaches into the house and showed me how to clean them and how to easily take the skin off them to be placed in bottles to be stored in the basement for the winter months. She saved some of the peaches and made a fresh peach pie for the entire family to eat at dinner time. She would make her pie crust and showed me how to roll out the dough made from scratch, slice the peaches into thin slices, and then cover them with a kitchen towel so the flies would not get on them.

Every time I smell a fresh peach, I am always taken back to this one experience in the garden. When someone asked me who my best friend was, I always said it was my mom.

My time with her wasn't only outdoors; it also reached back through our family's past.

Why My Ancestors Meant So Much to My Mom

When we weren't in the garden, we were uncovering roots of a different kind—names, stories, and journeys. I found other ways to spend time with my mom that none of the other kids like to do. On Saturday mornings, I would go down to the local Genealogy library, and we would search for our ancestry files. My mom wanted to find all the lost ancestors. Over the course of many years, spending time with her in the library, I learned about ancestors and other distant relatives. Mom would also share with me many other stories of my ancestors, from coming over on the Mayflower, to traveling on wagons across the plains, to even one of my grandpas who almost blew up the little one-room schoolhouse, after the teacher took his leather ball that was filled with gun powder and threw it into the fireplace.

Five Little Monkeys Jumping on the Bed: My First ER Visit

From quiet bedtime comforts to a memory that took a wild turn. One of my fondest experiences was when my mom read us a bedtime story. My favorite books were the *Curious George* series and *Five Little Monkeys Jumping on the Bed*. The sounds of my mom's voice were the best medicine for my breathing. I just fell right to sleep.

One day, while listening to my mom give piano lessons to one of her students, I was pretending to be like one of those monkeys. But instead of jumping on the bed, I took off the cushions from the couch, placed them on the floor, and started to jump. I was impressing myself by doing complete flips until I went too far, and my head hit the television. With the gushing blood coming out of my head, my oldest brother took off his white shirt and applied pressure to my head (he still reminds me to this day how I ruined his white shirt). He held me in the car as our mother drove us to the hospital, rushing up to the double doors of the entrance of the hospital. One of the medical staff quickly helped take me into a room where the doctor sewed the skin of my head back together, then applied the bandages just like those monkeys in the book. Moments like that only deepened my gratitude—and there's so much more I could say about her. If everyone had a mom like mine, there is no doubt that every child's dream would be fulfilled.

My First Painting: Finding Something to Hang It with

Shifting from memories of Mom to lessons and moments with Dad. Now, I could not do justice if I did not talk about my father as I did about my mother. I shared a lot about my father in my first book, *Health Dad Sick Dad*, but here are some more experiences that you have not heard.

When you stumble upon one of those things you love to do, my advice is to stick with it no matter what the response you get from others. For some reason, I was drawn to art at a very young age. Neither one of my parents was into art; my mother was into music, genealogy, and gardening. My father was into building machinery by welding and making wooden toys in his woodshop. I have never seen either parent paint or draw. Seeing a blank white paper and some crayons, I had to draw my masterpiece. When I was done, I could not find anything to hang it on the wall of my bedroom.

I went out into the shop, grabbed a hammer and a long nail, and went back into my bedroom and proceeded to hang my masterpiece. As I hit the nail with the hammer, little pieces of the wall fell to the floor. The wall was made of cinderblock and cement, not your typical sheet rock with wood studs. If I knew what a bomb shelter was at the time, that was my bedroom.

Once the masterpiece was on the wall, my excitement made its way out of the bedroom to the first person to show it off to. It happened to be my dad. I took him into the room and showed him my painting. Noticing all the cement fragments on the floor, he went over and tore the painting off the wall and told me never to use a nail or hammer on the wall again. It took many years before I picked up the medium to create something on the surface, but I never let that flame of creating something out of nothing go silent. I had planted a seed in my heart, and even though I was disappointed by my first masterpiece being thrown in the trash, I attempted to explore painting every once in a while, until I had to face my greatest challenge in life, where painting saved my life!

Praying in the Closet: The Secret Place Where I Found My Dad

Beyond work and rules, my father's example showed up in quieter, more personal ways. My father taught me many things in life. One of those things was how prayer and intuition help guide you in everyday life decisions. The very small house that we live in does not have much room for privacy. I recall, in the middle of the day, I went into the tiny closet off the living room to find something. There was my dad, on his knees in prayer. I slowly closed the door and went on doing something else. I don't know what that one prayer was about, but if it was any indication from the prayers before each meal, as the family sat down to eat, I could only imagine it had to do with somebody's welfare and needed help from above, or maybe my father just needed some answers to the questions he had. Inspired by what I saw, I decided to try it for myself.

Seeing my father on his knees praying to God, I told myself, "I'm going to put this to the test and see what happens." I was on a little league wrestling team called the Buckeyes. The end-of-the-season tournament was the next day, and I was in a bracket with an individual who had beaten me in the regular meetings. I prayed specifically that I would beat this person, and wouldn't you know, I beat him and took first place. I was hooked on prayer from that moment on; the only time in my life that I rested from praying was the time I needed it the most. Life is a lesson, and boy, did I learn from that experience. If there is one thing about prayer, it's free, and you don't have to stand in long lines in order to get it; all you have to do is either fall to your knees or create a simple thought on what you need at the moment.

Sunday Is a Day of Rest—Yeah, Right!

Faith shaped our lives, but so did the farm—and Sundays were no exception. Sundays were not a day of rest in our house; the cattle still needed to be fed. When I got the chance during Sunday school, I would arrange a gathering time to meet up at a local cow pasture after church and play a game of football. The Sunday school teacher did not like that I was interrupting the spiritual lesson while I was recruiting the other boys in the room to play football after church. It just seemed the only time I had to really play was on Sunday afternoons, or on a late Saturday night when we would all meet up and play kick the can or steal the flag at the local park.

Don't Be Afraid to Work: How I Approached Hard Work and Developed a Love for It

That same rhythm of responsibility shaped me early, and work became its own kind of classroom. If there was one thing that my dad taught me at a young age, it was the ability to work. Aside from helping my mom in the garden, I took my first paying job at the age of 10. I had my first full-time job during the summer. I would mow the lawns of the widowed ladies in the town. I would get paid a few dollars for the two- to three-hour service for mowing the yards.

Working for me was a time to talk with myself. I used work to mull over questions I had to figure out. While most people would see work as hard labor, I used it to dive deep into my questions of life. So now you know why I like washing dishes. Here are a few of the childhood jobs that I experienced.

Trigger Finger Takes on a Whole New Meaning

Here's the kind of summer job story that stuck with me—and why the title fits. At a young age, I had my own lawn mowing business. I would mow yards for older people in town and even a few cow pastures, but this is one experience I want to share with you.

One missed week led to a scene I'll never forget. I had missed a few weeks in between mowing on this one elderly lady's yard. The grass was taller than normal. As I was making a path down the orchard with the mower, I noticed out of the corner of my eye that the lady dropped one of her garden gloves, and before I could move out of the way, I mowed it over. Looking back to see the damage to the glove, I noticed that the glove was sitting face up, and the little finger, the ring finger, and the index finger were all gone. The only finger remaining was the middle finger. It was flipping me off. I spun that mower around and ran it over again, leaving no fingers. I then picked up the pieces of the glove after I finished the job. When I went to get paid, I handed the lady the glove that was so nicely dissected by the lawn mower. I asked her what I owed her for the glove. I never told her the whole story by mowing it over twice, but I took it personally when I got flipped off by the garden glove.

I Was Paid Not by Money but by a Cow. . .Say What?

Not every payment came in cash, and one surprised me more than even a tip could offer. My father had a good friend who spent his summer months up on a big ranch in Montana. He showed me what I needed to do and then left for the summer. When he came home in the fall to pay me for taking care of his yard, he went out to the barn, brought back a cow, and said, "Here is your payment." Yes, the cow was beautiful, and it had the biggest eyes, but what was I going to do with a cow? I was a teenage boy who could really use the money. I told him I would have to go home and talk to my dad. My dad was not a man of showing excitement, but he did have a smile on his face, and took the cow over to his barn, raised it, and fed it. That cow ended up giving birth to 4 more calves over the years, and it was probably the best payment for my work that I did while in my youth.

The work didn't stop there—farm life had its own lessons, some of them harsh.

Baling Black Hay Was a Thing for My Lungs

This is when I learned why timing mattered most as a farmer; it was the one job that God cursed, my father would say, and you were at the mercy of the elements. The only time I would see my father get angry in church was when someone would give an opening or closing prayer in the main meeting and pray for rain when my dad's hay was on the ground. He would say, I can't say amen to that prayer until my alfalfa hay is off the field. I soon learned why. It must have rained for days while my father's hay lay on the ground. When there was a break in the rain, he would have the tractors ready with the bailers, and when there was enough sun to dry out the hay, we would be baling that hay and getting it off the fields. That hay was so black, and there was no cabin on the tractor; I was breathing in all that black dust (molded hay). As I would go down one long row and then up another row, I stopped the tractor and stepped away from the dust. I could not catch my breath. Noticing something was wrong from a distant field where my father was, he jumped into the truck and rushed over to where I was. He helped me into his truck and rushed me back into town. He had me shower and rest, and I finally started to breathe. That was the last time that I was permitted to bale hay.

This was one of those life experiences to help you fine-tune what you really want in life. Staying on the farm and helping operate it, or going on to college and choosing a different profession, was the choice that I was facing. Just because I was permitted to bale hay does not mean I was permitted to work with the cattle.

Which brings me to another unforgettable chore—one you smell before you see.

The Smell of Burnt Flesh Could Make You Vomit

Saturdays meant projects, and spring meant working the herd up close. Saturday morning cartoons were short-lived in our house; somehow, my father would find projects to keep us busy all day. I think most of those projects were building, fixing, and repairing fences, structures, and various things on the farm. In the early spring, we would wean the cows. At first, I thought that was painful for the cows, and so I asked my dad, "Does weaning hurt the cows?" He chuckled and said, "No, weaning is when we separate the yearlings (one-year-old calves) from their mothers."

Herding the cows into the corral, my dad would get into his truck, which was basically held together with baling wire. Start tapping on the side of the door, and the cows would hear the sounds and start walking towards the truck. I then observed that there was a bale of hay in the back of the truck, but this time, instead of throwing out the hay in the field for them to eat, he just slowly drove the truck to the corral, and the cows followed. It was my job to walk behind the cows and make sure none of them decided to venture off, as we did not have any cow dogs or horses to help with the rounding up of the cattle. There was a reason why I wore my athletic shoes and not cowboy boots; I could run a lot easier with the shoes versus the boots.

Once we got all the cows separated from the yearlings, it was now time for branding (hot iron pressing it onto the hair and skin, leaving a permanent mark), fixing (taking a pocketknife and castrating the testicles), and vaccinating the yearlings. I oversaw loading up the calves by guiding them into a shoot. At first, getting kicked in the shins a few times caused me to find a way less painful means of pushing the calves up the shoot. I found a plywood board, and placed it in front of me, and pushed the calves up the shoot to get branded. I was ok with my job as the smell of burnt flesh coming from the calves and cows where my father and everyone else was working was much stronger, it was worth getting kicked in the shins every once in a while, as long as I did not have to smell that burnt flesh that would make you want to vomit.

The Milk Needs to Go into the Bucket Before the Cow Goes Out to the Pasture

Here's how a simple daily chore became a lesson I never forgot. There was a cow that my dad would milk every day; it was the milk that was used for baking, cooking, and drowning the cornflakes that I ate for breakfast. My grandmother would separate the cream from the milk and make butter. The cow was in an old barn at my grandmother's house. With time, as with anything on the farm, I was entrusted to do the job at hand. This time, it was milking the cow. There was a specific instruction: take the bucket of oats, allow the cow to smell it, lead the cow into the holding place, and put the bucket in front of the cow, then take the fresh, clean bucket and stool and start milking that cow as fast as you can. I was told that once that bucket of oats was empty, that cow was headed for the pasture, and there was nothing you could do to stop her. Of course, things didn't go as smoothly when my brother and I turned it into a game.

I wish the story of milking the cow could end here, but kids are kids. My brother decided to join me one day, and we did as instructed by my father, but this time we placed the bucket equally between us, and then proceeded to milk while that cow was eating her oats from her bucket. I was on one side, and my brother was on the other side. How my father milked that cow before the cow finished her oats was beyond my comprehension; maybe that is why he had forearms the size of Popeye.

Mischief won over discipline—and the consequence stuck with me. Noticing that my brother's foot was right there in my view, I started to squirt his shoe, and then his leg. Once he caught on to what I was doing, he started to do the same to me. We were soaked in milk, and that cow was headed out to the pasture as it had finished the bucket of oats. When we went to give the milk, my father investigated the bucket, and there was not even a cup of milk, but then he noticed milk dripping down our legs. It was the last time I milked that cow. From that point on, we drank powdered milk with everything. Sometimes lessons in life are painful, and every time I had a bowl of cornflakes with powdered milk reminded me of milking that cow and how I wish I could get a second chance.

Grave Digger by Day and Stock Boy by Night

Beyond farm chores, I chased work wherever I could find it—at all hours. There were many other jobs that I worked, from midnight into the early hours of the morning, stuffing advertisements in the local newspaper. I also responded to a help ad in the local newspaper when an elderly lady whose water turn was at 2 a.m.

and she could not change the head gates in the ditch and wade through the water to irrigate her yard. One other job my father got us into was taking care of the local cemetery. It was a good job that allowed me to bond with my older brother, who had died before I was born. I would take my time as I mowed around his grave; my thoughts would send messages to him, wondering what kind of brother he would have been to me. I would have to admit that there were times when I just wanted to get out of the cemetery, as it was just downright creepy and scary.

The only other job I will share with you until I landed the main job that I stayed with throughout high school was Mr. Maycock. He was an older gentleman who helped me buy my first NFL jacket. All I had to do was pick up all the apples and pears that fell out of the trees in his orchard. I got paid twenty-five cents a bucket. He even taught me how to fish. It took several years before I caught my first one, but he showed me how to stay persistent. Those odd jobs set the stage for something steadier—and safer than farm dust. It also taught life lessons that are not taught in the class-room, things like common sense, and work is good for you, and when you serve others, you make God smile.

With the help of my father, he had asked the owner of the local grocery store if there was anything I could do at his store. In a way, my father saw that I loved to work, but since the issues with my asthma and being on the farm, he did not want to have another scare.

At the age of twelve, I started working in the local grocery store, stacking the pop bottles that others would bring in. I would get them ready for the local soda pop companies to pick up when they dropped off the new batch of soda. I worked my way up to help-ing in the meat department and the produce department, stack-ing shelves, and working in the greenhouse during the spring and summer months. I would even oversee selling guns in the sporting goods part of the store, and eventually open and close the store.

Closing the store was a bit scary. My boss instructed me to empty the cash register, place the money in a bag, and bring it home to him. The only problem was that I was on a bike, and the dark alley that I had to ride through to get to the street was a bit scary for me. I would shut off all the lights to the store, set the alarm, and then quickly lock the door, ride to his house, drop off the money, and then ride back to my house.

I continued working at this little family store throughout my high school years. Working in the grocery store was a great experience for me. It taught me people skills, how to talk to people, and carry on a conversation while listening and observing what was being said.

Guardian Angels Are Always Surrounding Us, Even When I Walked on Water

I firmly believe we each have a guardian angel(s) that accompany our every step. We may not see them, but there are times in our lives when we look back and say, "How did this not happen?" Here's one of those times.

The very first school I attended was located by the city park, which had an outdoor swimming pool. It was the pool I spent most of my younger years at. In the wintertime, they did not drain the pool completely, and it would ice over when it got cold. Even with the colder temperatures, our recesses and physical education classes were outside no matter what the weather, as there was no gym in our school building. A group of us was playing kickball, and one of the students kicked the ball so hard that it went up and over the fence of the pool. It was the funniest sight to see, all of us lined up along the fence staring at this ball as it lay silently on the newly formed ice from the night before. One of the students yelled, "Hey Glen, since you are the smallest and lightest one here, why don't you climb the fence and get the ball? We will stay here and keep a lookout for any teachers."

Wanting to be the hero of the group, I climbed the fence, walked out to the end of the pool, looked at the best approach to walk out on the ice, and got the ball. After hearing the voices of the students say, "Hurry up, I think someone is coming," I just made the decision, walked out on the thin ice, grabbed the ball, threw it over the fence, and quickly climbed over the fence and joined the other students. How that ice never broke is beyond me. I just knew someone was watching over me that day.

Little League Baseball: The Reason Why I Don't Like Sports That Have Hard Objects Thrown at You

Sports brought a different kind of challenge—fear, and how to face it. One of the first real mental exercises that I faced was when I was playing Little League baseball. As long as I was playing in the outfield, I would catch anything. But batting was a different story; it seems the pitchers were twice as big as me, and throwing a hard object at me was a little bit scary. After being close to being hit, my fear of playing baseball was so intense that I wanted to quit. I did finish the season, and the team did very well. I felt so relieved that the season was over.

Then came the pressure to move up—and a test that rattled me.

The next year, I was pressured by my friends to play in the major league, and even the coach came to my house and gave me his sales pitch. The players were bigger, and my fear of batting was amplified. To help me, the coach brought in a pitcher who was a hard lefty from California to pitch to us. This did not help as I got smacked with that baseball. There was no time for reaction to move out of the way.

I was done with the major league, or so I thought. I did not give up on baseball, but I did go back to the minor leagues. The tables were turned; I was much bigger than the other players, and they even had me pitch a few games. I remember a player on the opposite team approaching the batter's box, but he stood on the very outskirts of the box. I could see in his face how scared he was to face me. This must have left an impression on me because I reflected on myself being so scared, and I did not want to scar this player for life. His helmet was bigger than his head, and the bat was longer than his body. He was shaking and trembling in fear as he approached the batter's box, hearing screams of encouragement from his team coming from the dugout, telling him, "You got this! Just step up to the plate and hit the ball." I did not throw the ball as hard to him as I did to the other players, and basically tossed it over the plate.

With some coaching and a shift in mindset, everything changed.

The coach asked me if I would like to come back to the majors. Still being afraid of batting, I told my mind that I was not scared, and I could hit the ball. They spent time with me at batting. They first just threw the ball over the plate so I could get used to hitting the ball, then the speed of the ball picked up, and with time, I was batting against the opposing team. I never struck out the rest of the season, and we went on to win the championship and were featured in the local 4th of July parade in our small town. I was also selected to be on the all-star team. My hitting streak continued while playing against the top team in the state. My highlight was going to the plate, and after hitting a triple and an RBI, the next time I went to the plate, they purposely walked me. From a scared little boy at the batter box to having the opposing pitcher purposely walk me, this was greater than hitting a home run because the pitcher saw my potential and did not want me to hit the ball, so the runner left on the base would score, giving us the win. The lesson stuck—and it stretched far beyond baseball.

What this taught me is that you don't grow in a comfort zone; it is when you are pushed beyond the comfort zone that growth takes place. I later learned the mind does not know the difference between excitement and fear, yet we let fear control us. Getting out of your comfort zone is just a mental exercise. The more you exercise your mind in the right way, the more growth you experience, and accomplishments and achievements follow.

School Lunch: Trying to Outsmart the Lunch Lady Is Not an Easy Task

A small cafeteria standoff taught me a bigger lesson. Since my mom would pay for school lunch, I would line up like everyone else in the lunch line and pray that there were no Beanie Weenies. I would also decline the cooked peas. One of the lunch ladies took notice that I did not have enough veggies on my plate. She asked me, "Are you not going to have the cooked peas?" I kindly replied that I don't like cooked peas, even though I would eat them out of the garden at home. I claimed that I only eat uncooked peas, thinking that she would never serve me peas again. The thought of eating fresh peas was much better; like eating them out of the pod, fresh from the garden, was a fun thing to do. The next day, I got that same lunch lady, and she said to me, "Peas?" I said, "No thanks," she said, "Oh no, not the cooked peas, but I have some uncooked peas." She caught my bluff and pulled out a bowl of uncooked peas from under the counter, and handed me a large bowl of uncooked peas fresh out of a can, double the size of the cooked peas. It was worse than eating cornflakes with powdered milk.

That moment followed me into the classroom and shaped how I approached tough subjects. Sometimes in life, it is just better to eat the cooked peas than try to outsmart your superiors. I applied this in school, as there were many subjects I did not like. Still, I made sure I would show an interest in the class and asked many questions; I pretended to like the subject because I knew it was harder for the teacher or professor to fail me if I showed interest in the subject. All I had to do for some of the classes was to pass so I could move on.

Reflection

Breathe through the hard nights and let chronic challenges teach endurance, empathy, and perspective. Be curious—track patterns, ask questions, and run small experiments that turn frustration into learning. Lean on your team, and let work be your classroom, where responsibility builds discipline, people skills, and confidence. Find the lesson in every mishap, adapt when life redirects, and steward small beginnings into momentum. Practice faith and a focused mindset, step outside your comfort zone, control what you can, own consequences, and respect mentors. Keep humor and gratitude close, build character through service, and persist with patient effort until breakthroughs come.

Bottom line: life will surprise you—rain on hay, ice underfoot, a curveball at the plate—so meet it with curiosity, preparation, and flexibility; lean on your people, train your mind, work hard, and keep your humor. When you can't control the wind, adjust your sails; when you can, row with all your might—and let each unexpected moment become a stepping-stone.

CHAPTER 2

Good Luck Getting into College

The stars come nightly to the sky.
The tidal waves come to the sea;
Nor time, nor space, nor deep, nor high,
Can keep my own away from me.

– John Burroughs

My Very First Surgery Was on a Cow Heart

I had just walked into school that day. It was just another boring day; I found my desk and sat down. Trying to pay attention to the teacher in school was like putting on a pair of ballet shoes and performing the Nutcracker. For one, it did not make any sense to me to be stuck in a room and learn subject matters that I would never apply in life. And then suddenly some of the townspeople came into our classroom with black bags, and my eyes got really big. They placed the bags on the table, and you could smell something dead inside, but we couldn't tell what it was. We were all anticipating what was in the bags.

Then the teacher gave the green light, and those people from the town started to open each bag, and out fell cow guts and cow heart and everything that had just lived the day before. And here it was, right in front of me, they placed a razor blade on the table. I was waiting for instructions, but the teacher and the townspeople were trying to do damage control on the students who were ready to vomit and squirming in their chairs in complete disgust. Some students even walked away from their desks. I, on the other hand, grabbed the razor blade and went right for the heart, sinking the blade deep into the heart. I discovered what was inside. It was probably the only time I actually paid attention in school, other than dissecting the frog that smelled of formaldehyde. Little did I know at that time in the sixth grade that it would not be my last experience with dissecting. Had I known I would one day be scrubbing in on an open-heart surgery, then I would have paid a little more attention to the teachers.

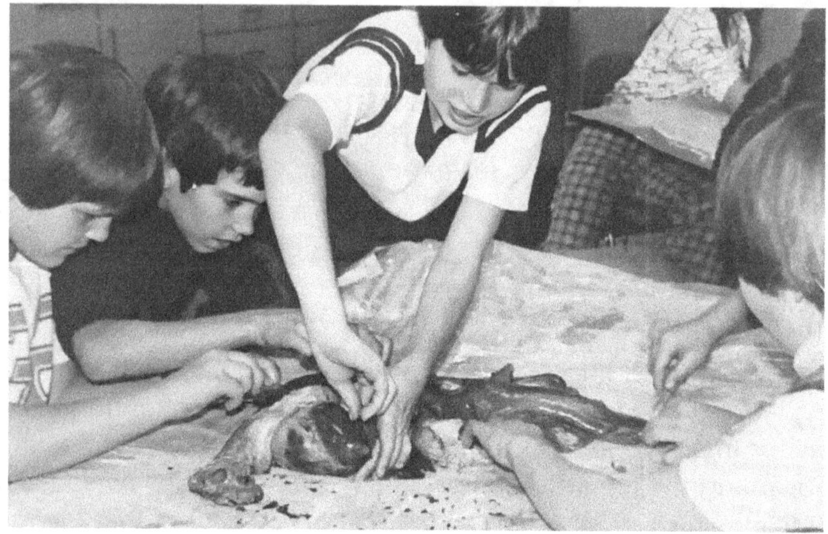

6th Grade dissection of a cow heart.

From Dissecting a Dead Organ to Operating on a Living Thing

One Saturday morning, I went with my dad to the farm. Today we were castrating piglets. There seemed to be hundreds of them as I watched my dad take out his pocketknife, grab the piglet, slice open the scrotum and tease out the testicle, cutting it off and doing it to the other one, and getting up off the piglet and letting the piglet run off, and then off to the next one. He looked over at me and noticed that I was just observing him, and he said, "Hey, if you want to be a surgeon, you'd better learn how to cut skin." He handed me his pocketknife and said, "Do it." I sat on the little piglet, took the pocketknife, made the skin incision, teased out the testicle, removed the other one, and went off to the next one. It truly was my first surgery on a living thing.

First Paper I Turned in: "D" Did Not Mean I Failed!

Junior high was a little more difficult than elementary school. I did not have Google, the internet, or a handheld phone to ask Siri for help with any questions. There was no AI or all this technical stuff we have today. Any report that needed to be turned in to school had to be handwritten, or if you were lucky enough to have a typewriter, you could type your reports. Any information that needed research was found in books found in the home or at the library. Here is just one of the experiences I had with one of my teachers at the beginning of my junior high school.

I remember I had an assignment to write my own made-up story of a mythological character. My mind went right to work, and I developed two characters, Thunder and Lightning. It was two brothers, one was thunder, and the other was lightning, and they worked together. I thought I had created a rather spectacular storyline. My only spell check was my mother. I was so happy to turn this paper in, but when I received it back, it had a big red D on the front of the cover page. It reconfirmed to me that I did not like school at all, and English was one of my hardest subjects.

At the time, I struggled with reading and writing, even though I loved to create. As disappointing as this D on my paper was, little did I know that this one D was another seed I planted deep into my soul to help me later in my life. One day, I would learn that D stood for doctor. That early sting of a red D didn't stop me—it pushed me to look for purpose beyond the classroom, which is how I first crossed paths with the high school counselor.

I Need This Fixed ASAP!: Meeting the High School Counselor

I applied for the position of equipment manager for the varsity football team. The team that was poised to win it all for the state title. The head football coach, who was also the high school counselor, was the person who determined who was going to be his manager for the football season. I so wanted to get out of the classroom and knew if I could get this position, I would be traveling with the team during school hours, plus it was a position that gave responsibility, which I eagerly searched for. I was excited to learn that I was picked to be one of those managers. It was my job to make sure all the equipment was working, from the helmets to the footballs, and to make sure the medicine box was filled and ready to go for game day.

On game day, when a player came off the field with blood running down their face, or a finger that was dislocated, or even a player who got their bell rung by a head-on collision with another player, I knew where the bandages were, the smelling salts, and the tape to put the finger back in place. There were no sport trainers; the only people on the field to handle these situations were the assistant coach and me. As for an equipment failure, it was all up to me to fix it and get the player back on the field.

Every day I stepped into the locker room for practice or for game day, my stomach was in a knot. I feared the head coach more than I feared the what-ifs. Did I get yelled at? Yes, but everyone else also got yelled at. Did I have things thrown my way, adding to the frustrations on the field? Yes, but I stuck with it. We ended up being the State Football Champions that year.

I had no idea that three years later, I would be standing in the coach's office listening to him give me counseling advice after taking my American College Test (ACT). What I will tell you is that he was no different as a counselor than he was as a football coach. Not all my lessons came under Friday night lights; some arrived in the back row of a classroom, where a heater, a window, and a pocketful of mischief kept me company.

Pine Nuts Are Not Suitable for the Classroom Heater

When I was in school, I would purposely sit in the very back row of the class. It was where the baseboard heater was, and it was close to the windows, so I could look outside and wish I were out there rather than being inside.

On the days it was cold, the teacher would tell me to turn the heater on. There was a period between the good weather and the cold weather; it was also pine nut season. I loved eating pine nuts. The only bad thing about it was what to do with the shells. I emptied my pockets filled with pine nut shells into the space heater. We were not supposed to eat in class, but I had to do something with the shells. I couldn't throw them away in the trash, so I emptied my pockets into the space heater. The teacher at the front of the room said, "Glen, can you please turn on the heater? It's cold in here." I pretended not to hear him, but after he repeated it three times and his voice was getting louder each time, I leaned over and reached my hand into the heater and turned it on. And then I immediately jumped under my desk, as did everyone else, as those pine nut shells became projectiles.

So why am I telling you this? Yes, any student who got in trouble had to make the long walk to the counselor's office. Yes, the same man who was the football coach. I dreaded that walk as the teacher told me to go to the office. I said many prayers in my mind as I walked down the hallway, hoping Mr. Monsen would not be there. It was my lucky day when the secretary told me that the counselor was gone for the morning. It was up to the secretary to punish me. The only thing she could think of was sending me to my mom's special education class. I said to her, "Do you really have to do that?" I was acting like it was a scary idea, but inside, I was jumping for joy to go now and spend time with my mom.

I found that spending time in my mom's office was much better than spending time in my classes. Some of the teachers caught on to my intentions, and they just enrolled me in special education. When my mother found out about my intentions and realized I did not need special education, she unenrolled me, and I had to go back to the classes that I did not want to be in.

Mr. Monsen: The School Counselor/Head Football Coach/Most Feared Man on Campus

No matter what I did, I could not escape Mr. Monsen, the most feared man on campus. He has so many titles; not only was he the head football coach, but he was also the counselor and the vice principal. To make matters worse, he was the basketball coach for the boys' 7th and 8th grades. He was a no-nonsense, foul-mouthed, hard-nosed person who did not have an ounce of compassion in his body. In the 7th grade, I witnessed two boys getting into a fight. What did Mr. Monsen do? He took both of those boys, placed them in an area so everyone could see, put boxing gloves on them, and they had to fight until neither one of them had enough strength to lift their arms to throw another punch.

In eighth grade, Mr. Monsen was my P.E. teacher and my basketball coach. One day, he decided to have us run for the entire hour of the class. I could hardly breathe with a triggered asthma attack, and I was not permitted to stop. I had to keep pace with the other boys. I ended up missing school for a week because I was so sick with my asthma, and it took a whole week to get it under control. Once I got my strength back, I went back to school, and yes, I had to face Mr. Monsen in P.E.

Because I loved basketball so much, I did not let him stop me from playing the game. This time, I put an inhaler in my knee-high stocking, and when I felt an asthma attack coming on, I would sneak a puff or two without anyone seeing, or so I thought. I tried out for the basketball team and made it, and became one of the starters on the team. Running on those dirt roads and dribbling a basketball paid off.

"Kick Him Out!" Yelled the Opposing Team: Playing Basketball Against Our Rival School

With my spot on the team and my inhaler hidden, the real tests came under bright lights and louder crowds. One of the games we had to play was against our rivals, the Delta Rabbits. They, too, were a good team, but their school was known for wrestling. Basketball was not a high priority for the school, but they did put together a team that was very hungry for a win. Because I took a lot of self-pride in my ball-handling abilities and the fear of sitting on the bench with Coach Monsen, I did everything in my power to stay on the court. I learned how to block out his yelling.

The game was going back and forth, then a player stole the ball from me and took off to the opposite end of the court. Worried about being benched or getting yelled at by the coach, my first reaction was subtly taking out the player's legs as he had a few steps on me, and I knew I could not get in front of him to stop him from scoring a basket. Right then, in mid-court, I got close enough to him that I pretended to go for the ball with my foot and tripped him as he slid face-first down the court. I was waiting for the referee to blow his whistle to call a foul on me and maybe even a technical foul. If the player only knew what my coach was like, he would have had compassion for me. As the referee blew his whistle and signaled traveling, we got the ball back. I briefly looked over to the coach and noticed the first sign of a smile on his face. I felt bad for the player and did not mean to hurt him, but all I could hear from the crowd was the chant of kick him out, get him out. The love for basketball grew with each year. I did feel bad for what I did, but I also never had anyone steal the basketball from me in all the games I played.

My Dream to Play College Basketball Was Sidelined Because I Did Not Play Football

Figuring out a way to control my asthma on the court, it was now my dream to go on to college and play basketball. I trained all year round; I made the basketball team during my freshman and sophomore years. Even though I started on the JV team, I knew for sure I would make varsity in my junior year. I even went to the summer basketball camp at BYU. I continued my running on dirt roads, dribbling a basketball, and would shoot foul shots on my dirt court at home. I was excited to play varsity basketball. What was even more exciting was that we had a coach who was part of the Phi Slama Jama Houston Cougars college basketball team, which lost in the last second to NC State. But even the best preparation can't guarantee the outcome that lives in your heart.

I did not make the team in my junior year. I was told they did not want someone using an inhaler on the court. This made me even more determined to make the team in my senior year. I was also told that if I wanted to play basketball, I had to play football. Because I loved basketball so much, I went to the first day of football season. I even had a jersey with my name on it with the number 1.

I ended up leaving after that first day; my heart was not in it. I went and joined the cross-country team instead. We ended up going to state that year, and I was the first senior to run at a state cross country in our school history. A few of the football players told me that because I chose not to play football, the coaches would see to it that I did not play basketball. Still, hope has a way of pulling you back to the gym, even when the odds—and the coaches—aren't on your side.

When basketball season came along, I showed up to the basketball tryout and knew what I was up against at the end of the few-day tryouts. They posted the team outside the gym door. I started at the top of the list and moved my finger down the list, and could not find my name. So I started up the list from the bottom with my finger, and still could not find it. I was not even listed as an alternate player. All I dreamed about was basketball; it was my everything. Instead of going to class, I went back home, pulled the bed sheets over my head, and tried to fall asleep, thinking it was only a bad dream. That was short-lived as my mother walked into my room and proceeded to say, "Get out of bed, and go back to school. Do not let this one thing define you. Do not let one person stop you from doing something great." Her words were firm, and so was my next test—walking back into classrooms taught by the very men who cut me.

Her tone of voice said everything. I went back to school and walked into class, where I tutored under classmates; the class "Geography" just happened to be one of the assistant basketball coaches' classes. As I walked into the class and sat at my desk, the teacher then got up and walked out of the class, and did not return.

My true test was having to face the head coach in my typing class. As I walked into his class, he was nowhere to be found; he did not show up to class. In the middle of all that disappointment, loyalty showed up where I least expected it–among friends and family.

My best friend in school, who made the team, quit the next day. I asked him why he quit, and he said, "Football is my love, and I was only going out for basketball for you." I felt bad because I knew football was important to him, and I felt a little guilty for not finishing the football season for him. That day, the coaches called a team meeting. They said one SOB had already quit, then proceeded to challenge the team, "Is there anyone else who wants to quit?" One player raised their hand; the coach pointed to the door at the back of the room and told them to leave. When I noticed my brother was home early from basketball practice, he admitted to having left the team and explained to me what had happened. This brother and I had had our differences since we were little, but I gained a lot of respect and love for him when he stood up and walked out that day.

Losing a dream hurt–but what I took from it has lasted far longer than any season.

There are a lot of lessons learned from this one event. True friends will always have your back no matter what, and if you love what you do and still don't get to finish it, it is not a failure; there is something to learn, so keep persisting in your goals and desire. And don't let one person define who you are. "Don't let idiots ruin your day!" With those lessons packed away, I turned toward the next milestone–the one that could open doors beyond high school.

Taking the ACT for the First Time

In my junior year, we were told that if we took the College entrance examination, we would get two extra points added if we took it in our junior year. There was no prep course offered; the only thing that was given to us with any notice was the date and time of when the test could be taken. In the spring of my junior year, I had a track meet in St. George, Utah. I figured I would just stay the night and then take the test at the college the next day. I got up the next morning, went to the testing center, took the test, and then had to wait several weeks for the results. All I could think about was the one question that asked me what kind of mechanism a frog sweats. In my mind, it made no sense as to whether a frog sweats or not. I wonder how I fared with the other questions on the test.

"Good Luck Getting Into College," The Guidance Counselor Advised Me

A few weeks later, the ACT reports came out. As my classmates were getting their results and sharing their scores, I was wondering why I hadn't gotten mine. Sitting in my English class, the loudspeaker said, "Glen Robison, please report to the office." Sitting in the back row, I made my way up to the front of the room to exit through the door. My classmates were saying, "Oh, Glen's in trouble again," while pointing at me. Only the bad kids got called down to the office. Still, I was used to it by now, so it did not bother me what others were saying.

That summons wasn't about trouble—it was about a score that would try to define me.

As I approached the office, the secretary said, "Mr. Monsen will see you now." His door was half opened, tapping on his door with my knuckle in a very soft manner, he said, "Come in." As I went to sit down, he said, "No need to sit. This will not take long."

He said, "Glen, I got your results on your ACT exam, and you just got the lowest score in the entire state of Utah. You are in the bottom 5th percentile in the nation. You can be a farmer like your dad or go to vol tech school, but good luck getting into college. Now get back to class." His words stung, but they also lit a fire I didn't know I had.

As I was walking out of his office and heading back to class, my steps were a little slower, and my thoughts were a little faster. I was saying to myself, "What in the hell is Vol Tech school, and there is no way I could farm like my dad due to my asthma." It was right then that I decided to go to college and **Show Him** that he was wrong.

I think, looking back on things, this event defined my course in life. I had been told many times that "you can't do this," like my art teacher in his class, or "you can't do that," like play basketball by the coaches. You're too weak and not strong enough, according to the physical education teachers. You can't read or write, according to my English teachers. Then I said to myself, "What score did I get?" having not looked at the results. At the top, it said my cumulative score was seven. When I started to ask other students what they got on their test, they would say, "Oh, I got a 21 or a 24"; some would say, "I got a 17," or the lowest one that is closest to my score was 14. I kept silent about what I got. I decided to retake the test in my senior year. When I retook the test, to my surprise, I got the same score–seven–, and this was without the two points given as a bonus, so I actually got a five the year before and a seven my senior year. If the front door to college seemed shut, I started looking for side doors.

Finding Other Means to Get into College

One of the things I did to help my chances of making it into college was running for student body president, but I missed the election by thirteen votes. I was nominated to be the class president; this did not require a certain grade point average (GPA), all it required was passing grades. I also got more involved with FFA (Future Farmers of America) and held leadership positions. It was my hope that one of these leadership positions could help me get into college. When leadership alone wasn't enough, I tried another path—the military route.

ASVAB (Armed Services Vocational Aptitude Battery): Another Failed Exam

Figuring I would take another avenue to get into college, I looked at the military. There was another required test that all seniors had to take, which was the ASVAB (Armed Services Vocational Aptitude Battery) test. It was a test for eligibility into the military.

Every senior took the test, but only two of us were called back into the National Guard commanding officer's office. The commander said to my friend Jeff, "We think you have a good chance of qualifying for an officer scholarship. You're so close so we would like to have you take the test again," then he turned to me and said, "You got the lowest score that we have seen; we think you purposely tanked the test so you would not have to go into the military." In a way, it was like a slap in my face for being non-patriotic. The officer then said, "I am giving you both a second chance. We would like to have you come back and retake the test."

My friend looked at me and said, "The last place I want to go is in the military." In my mind, all I wanted to do was to make it into college, and if that meant going into the military, then I would do it. We both agreed to retake the test.

We showed up at the National Guard building on a Saturday. The building looked like it had been bombed in World War II, paint falling off the walls, the lights were dark, and it was as cold as a freezer. I know because we had Little League basketball games in that building. The officer showed us where we would take the test. It was in a room that looked like a place for interrogation. As we finished the test and handed it to the personnel, he said, "We will be getting back in touch with you."

My friend did not get the score that they were looking for. As for me, I got the same score, and they were not interested in me. With tests behind me and doors still closing, the next gatekeepers came to us—college recruiters with clipboards and opinions.

Holding Back the Laughs from the Recruits of the University's Personnel

In our senior year, we would have universities and colleges come in to try to recruit us for their schools. I can tell you they did not try to recruit me, but only laughed at me when they saw my ACT scores. One of those universities even told me I would never step foot on their campus. They may have laughed then, but I will **Show Them** who got the last laugh.

The only college that did not laugh at me was Snow College; they told me they did not require the ACT to enter their school. They helped me find scholarships to go to school there. Yes, I did get a scholarship to go to college. I got a $200 scholarship from the leadership position with the FFA and a $50 scholarship for being class president. Even though the total amount of my scholarship did not add up to buying a book for any of my classes, it gave me the gas money to drive to the campus and start college. My work at the local grocery store provided the rest of the money for housing, food, and tuition that I saved while working during high school.

Reflection

This chapter of my life traces my path from a struggling student to a determined young adult, turning setbacks into stepping stones. A red D on a mythology paper, the fear and grit learned under Coach/Counselor/Vice Principal Mr. Monsen, and even a pine-nut prank pushed me beyond the classroom and into responsibility as a varsity football equipment manager. I managed asthma to keep playing the sport I loved, learned to face hard voices without letting them define me, and discovered that even when dreams—like making varsity basketball—don't pan out, character and perseverance can still win the day. The lowest ACT score, an ASVAB disappointment, and recruiters' laughter could have closed my future. Instead, they fueled my resolve to find another route—small scholarships, steady work, and the open door at Snow College.

Along the way, true friends and family showed up when it counted, reminding me I wasn't alone. The life lessons are clear: don't let one person or moment define your worth; use setbacks as fuel; when the front door closes, find a side door; preparation matters, but perseverance matters more; and keep your humor and hope—don't let idiots ruin your day.

In the end, the obstacles of my youth became training for the future, teaching me to create opportunities, work hard, and believe in a bigger story. Success isn't avoiding failure; it's moving forward in spite of it.

CHAPTER 3

Defying the Odds

For life is the mirror of king and slave.
'Tis just what you are and do.
Then give to the world the best you have,
And the best will come back to you.

— Madeline Bridges

A Little College Allowed Me to Prove Myself After a Disastrous ACT Score

After finally finding a college that fits my unique situation, the next step was adjusting to life on and around campus. Finding a school that did not take college entrance examinations was a challenge; there was only one school that I found in the entire state of Utah that did not require the ACT as a prerequisite. I chose to go to Snow College, which was a few hours away from home and far enough that I would have to make choices for myself and learn to live on my own. The good thing was that my brother was going to the same college. Once settled nearby, the daily rhythms of small-town college life began to reveal both charm and surprise.

I lived just off campus, but close enough to walk to school each day. Some days, I woke up to farmers herding their sheep down the main road on the college campus. The most shocking thing I encountered was roommates; they had very different personalities, and something I had to deal with. The other thing, the teachers really did not care if I showed up to class or not. It was completely different from high school. In high school, there was a school police force that would call your house to find out where you were if you did not show up to school. The schools were only concerned about the pupil count to get their state funding, and the colleges were only concerned that you paid them your tuition. Those early observations set the stage for a lesson I wouldn't forget—one that arrived in the most unexpected way.

Be Aware of Land Mines Hidden in the Grass Fields While Getting to Class

One morning brought that warning to life. I got up early and darted off to school. I like my geography class and wanted a good seat so I could listen to the instructor. As I took a short-cut across the sports fields, I happened to look down, and just before I could move out of the way, I stepped right into a fresh dog poop. It took more time to rub my shoes off than I expected. I made it to class and found a seat more in the back of the room. I thought I had all of the dog poop off my shoe, but I noticed that everyone started to look at the bottom of their shoes, and then they silently shrugged their shoulders to tell everyone that it wasn't them. I followed suit and looked at the bottom of my shoes, and just shrugged my shoulders to say nope, it was not me either. Beyond these everyday setbacks, the deeper challenge came from my academic load and habits.

The biggest mistake I made was taking a very loaded course of classes because I did not have very good study habits. I never step foot in the college library and did all my studies at the apartment. As the semester was winding down, I did make a few trips back home to have my mom help me with my English class. She would read the chapter to me and help me understand what the assignment was asking for. How I made it this far without knowing how to read was an embarrassment, but thank goodness for my mom and her willingness to help me with my assignments. As grades reflected the strain, a familiar voice from the past began to echo louder.

Self-Doubt Creeping in After Being Put on Academic Probation

I started to feel the high school counselor was right in his statement that I was not meant for college. Even though I did make it into college, I was getting D's and C's. I was put on probation for failing to keep up the required academic requirements for college, and my time at Snow College was short-lived. I could say I lost my scholarship, but the money was already gone with one book and gas money to get to school. Faced with uncertainty, I chose a different path—one focused on faith and service.

Going Away for Two Years: A Time I Devoted All to the Lord

I put my papers in to go and serve the Lord for two years. I was called to go to the Seattle, Washington mission. This meant I would leave my family and friends and go to a place that I had never been before and tell people about Jesus Christ. On the first day of my mission, I met this very large missionary. His name was Elder (a title that signifies they are acting as ordained ministers of the church and are representing it officially, regardless of their age) Ngatuvai from Tonga. He said you pronounce it "not too wide," but after seeing him eat a banana by biting off the end and squeezing it out the back end, I was a little intimidated. The mission was a major growth time for me, from leadership positions to helping people of all kinds. Day by day, the mission became a training ground for resilience and perspective.

The mission was another gym moment for my mind; it seems to be exercising every day, dealing with companions, having people yelling at you, and even being bitten by a dog. I often wondered why people were so rude and tried to run me off the narrow roads when all I was doing was telling people about Jesus Christ. Leaving the mission made me realize that, really, there are no strangers, just friends I haven't met yet. People in general are good, and there are good people in all races, religions, and cultures. The two years that I spent gave me the confidence to talk to people and the ability to see my true potential in the midst of doubters. In God's eyes, he only sees greatness in everyone. With that growth came habits that anchored my days.

If there ever was a time for personal growth, it was within these two years. I must have driven my companions up the wall. Every time we left the apartment, we prayed. I also prayed at night, in the morning, and throughout the day. One quiet morning on the road, those prayers met a sudden test.

This one particular morning, we had got up early and were traveling across the city. There was little traffic on the road. I was driving in the middle lane, and there was a car up in front of me to my right and one just behind me to my left. I noticed that a vehicle further up the road had hit an object in the road that sent it bounding down the road right into our path. I could not move to my left, nor could I move to the right. I had no time to swerve or stop the vehicle, which would cause a chain reaction on the freeway. The only thing left I could do was allow this object to come smashing into our front windshield. What followed felt like protection in the midst of danger.

After finding a safe place to pull over, I noticed the object had hit directly between my companion and me. We had glass in our pockets, and the rearview mirror was knocked into the back of the vehicle. The glass was completely shattered with a very large hole in the middle of the front windshield. It was a silent miracle to me to pray for safety in my travels. I still pray every single day when I leave my place. I always pray for guidance to keep me safe while traveling. As the most demanding chapter of service drew to a close, the weight and reward of those years came into sharp focus.

After Two Years in the Trenches, the Last Day of My Mission Was Upon Me

On the last day of my mission, the mission president's wife made a lovely breakfast for Elder Ngatuvai and me. We both decided to stay a month longer and did not go home with the group that we went out with. It was a hard day for me. I had just spent the last two years with no vacation, no breaks, just telling people about Jesus Christ. The personal growth I experienced was what I needed. My two suits and the torn, worn-out shoes that I went out in needed to be retired from all the rainstorms and bike rides. I had given it my all, and there was nothing more in the tank to give. Elder Ngatuvai and I walked off the plane to greet our family after two long years of not seeing them. It was a joyful reunion. It was not the last day we would see each other; there were great things planned for us in the upcoming months ahead.

With the mission complete, the next frontier was education and a chance to rewrite my academic story.

Two-year Christian mission first time I met Corona.

The Education of Persistence: Ricks College – Time to Redeem Myself

After taking two years off from schooling, I wanted to reconsider going back to college. My ACT score was still fresh in my mind, but this time, I believed that once I got into college, it would be a different story. As paths converged again, brotherhood and opportunity pointed us toward the same destination.

Do you remember "Not Too Wide"? Well, we ended up going to the same college, we no longer used our "elder" name, and used our first name. Elder Ngatuvai will now be known as Corona. I did not want to go back to Snow College; it just felt like there were more opportunities in a new college. Corona was heavily recruited for the football team. How could he not–6'3" and 330 with a body fat of less than 10 percent? We made such a great connection that we became brothers from a different mother.

I decided to join Corona at Ricks College in northern Idaho. With a few phone calls from my mission president, he helped us find a place to live. He made some connections to get the process started to become enrolled in school for the upcoming school year in the fall. Before classes began, a first look at campus tested our transition from mission life to student life.

First Visit to Ricks College: Did the Rules of the Mission Still Apply to Us?

Just shortly after being home from the mission, it was a major culture shock for me. I was no longer in a white shirt and tie that I wore on a daily basis, and I had someone with me 24/7 now in street clothes. I also had the freedom to go places without anyone by my side. I met up with Corona, and we drove up to Rexburg, Idaho, in early spring. Corona did most of the driving, as he said you could drive around his entire Island in Tonga in less than a few hours. He seemed to enjoy driving, especially without constantly seeing the same thing.

That first trip mixed funny reminders of mission rules with the practical steps of enrollment. I'll never forget that first trip to Ricks College. As we were making our way to the road that led to the campus, these two girls stepped out in front of us, asking for a ride. I looked at Corona, and he looked at me, and we drove around them. We had never had a girl in our car for two years, and when we realized what we had done, we both laughed. One of the mission rules was that we could not have anyone else in our vehicles other than our companion, something to do with insurance and potential lawsuits. Corona met with the football coach, and he made me go and talk to the basketball coach. When we finished all the paperwork that was required of us to enroll in school, we drove back home to Utah. I went and finished working in the grocery store and helped my brother with his meat-packing plant. Since I did not have a scholarship to go to college, I had to work to pay for my schooling.

With the logistics in motion, the next step was guidance—finding someone who believed in what could come next.

Meeting My Advisor for the First Time: You Can Do It!

I met up with my new advisor, Dr Larry Hibbert. He was waiting for me in his office. I expressed to him that I wanted to do something in the medical field. He looked over my transcript from Snow College and, noticing my ACT score, he said, "I don't care what you did in your past; what I care about is what you do from this point on. If you want to go into medicine, then do it." His words resonated in my ears. I needed to hear those positive words: "You can do it." He went on to say, "You first need to explore all areas of interest, from education to medicine, then once you find that one thing that makes you excited, go for it."

Encouraged and focused, I stepped into the classroom with a new approach.

Starting My New Chapter in Schooling

Sitting in my American Heritage class, the first thing I noticed was that this one class was larger than my entire high school enrollment. One of the first things that was different was that I sat closer to the front of the classroom than the very back. I found there was less distraction from other students, and I could really focus on what the professor was saying. To match my ambitions, I reshaped how and where I learned.

With having multiple roommates, I quickly found places where there was complete silence to study, like the library and an empty classroom. I still had difficulty concentrating and focusing when I studied, so I needed complete silence, with no movements when I studied. I knew I had to study twice as long as most students, and I did not have my mom around to help me read my class assignments. I was truly on my own. The other thing I did was sign up for free tutoring. I needed all the help I could get. I also made sure I enrolled in next semester's Study Skills class.

Alongside new study habits, I needed steady work to keep the lights on.

Because I needed money to pay for my schooling for tuition, living, and food, I was able to land a job as a security guard at the gym. I was on the police force, telling students to put on their goggles while playing racquetball and kicking students out of the gym for not wearing the proper attire. It was a good-paying job that most students wanted, and having the keys to the building was a bonus. I could unlock any room in the gym and go places that most students did not know about. That job also created small moments that reminded me how much trust matters.

I remember one night when I was working security, it was raining hard, and a female student had to get back to her place, but did not want to run across campus in the rain. I gave her the keys to my car and told her just to bring them back after it stopped raining. Talk about being trustworthy; I didn't even know her, but she took the keys, and she did bring my keys back with the car later that night, after it stopped raining.

Even with sports opportunities nearby, I chose a different path and found closure with the past. I never did try out for basketball; I felt going after the great dream of becoming a doctor was more on my mind. I wanted to be a doctor and find a cure for asthma, so I just put my head into the books and started the journey. I happened to run into my old high school coach, who was in town coaching a college from southern Utah. I thanked him for cutting me from the basketball team. I told him it gave me the extra drive to become something someday. That was the last time I ever talked to him. He went on to coach Division I basketball.

Forgiving him was long overdue; walking out of the gym that day gave me peace of mind. Sacrifices became routine as I kept my focus and funded the dream.

The rest of the school year, I remained focused on my schooling and kept up with my grades. I did not travel back home as much. The one time I did go home was for Christmas. I needed some money to make it back to college, so I sold my leather jacket and shotgun. The only time I went back home was during my summer break when I worked for the government as an Initial attack wildland firefighter for the summer.

The one thing that helped me the most was the Study Skill class. I recall missing class one day; I never missed class, but somehow, I did that day. I got a call from my teacher, and I thought, "Wow, they really do care whether or not I am in class or not." The professor asked if I would be interested in working in the Study Skill Lab. I said I would love that. I started next semester and helped other students perfect their study skills while also working on mine at the same time. With momentum from the previous year, the next chapter brought new living arrangements and renewed focus.

Second Year at Ricks College: A Major Milestone Reached

I made it through my first year with all passing grades, and now I am starting my second year of school. A new place and new roommates, I was still roommates with Corona and now Patrick, my Catholic Friend. Corona continued to help me in school with subjects that were difficult for me, like Math and physics.

Day by day, structure and steady effort became the backbone of my routine. I continued working at the study skills lab. In my spare time, I would be studying in the library or a quiet room with no distractions. Life with roommates, of course, came with its own brand of problem-solving.

Solving the Dishwashing Problem in College

If any of you have ever had roommates in college, you will get a laugh out of this one. I got so tired of doing all the dishes that were left in the sink by my roommates, so I went down to the local furniture store and asked for the biggest box they had. They brought out a box for a washing machine. I took it back to the apartment, placed it outside the front door, and then took all the dirty dishes and threw them in the box. My roommates knew I was serious and was no longer their personal dishwasher, and if they wanted to eat, they had to wash their own dishes. Problems solved, and all it took was thinking outside the box, no pun intended.

Finding a Balance Between Schooling and Pleasure

By this time, I knew I wanted to go into medicine, and so most of my classes were now in Pre-Medicine, but what field of Medicine was still to be determined. Even with my head in the books, I made space for occasional dates.

I had to work on my skills of asking the girls out; unfortunately, those skills were not taught in any class, but only found through experience. I thought it was all about being creative. Still, I should have just stuck to the simple phone and asked, "Would you like to go with me?"

On one occasion, I went and bought a ten-pound bag of popcorn from the movie theater. It took me all day to fill up close to 10 large garbage bags. One of the roommates of the girl I wanted to ask out let me into their apartment, and we covered the entire living room 2 to 3 feet deep with popcorn. In the middle of all this popcorn was a hidden message, and then I taped a message to the front door with directions. Well, that one backfired on me, as they were so upset about all the kernels that they were picking up for weeks. Obviously, she said no.

Not every invitation went my way—and sometimes I had to respond with care.

"Answer To a Date" by Glen N Robison

It was Tuesday, the week before preference, and I received a message in a jar. A girl had asked me to go to the dance. She left no name or address, just a social security number. The next day, I went to the library to find out who this person was. It took me quite some time to respond to her invitation. I realized that I wasn't creative enough, so I came up with this poem. I didn't want to hurt her by saying no. I've never had to say no before, and it was hard. This is how I responded to her message:

I've tried to be creative. And I tried to be on time.
But all I could come up with was your answer in a rhyme.
I'm honored that you'd ask me to this Friday's preference dance.
I'd really like to go with you. I don't have the chance.
So please don't be offended. Cause my work times aren't right!
Let's smile and think positive; we'll both make dough that night.

Time Will Pass—Will You?

In one of my anatomy classes, there was a sign that hung above the clock that said, "Time will pass, will you?" Every time I walked into class, I would look at the clock. The main reason was that there were no cell phones back then, and I wanted to see how much time I had before class started. Every time I saw that clock, I would see that sign. It was stuck in my head like a bad song you just heard on the radio.

Not every lesson was easy to sit through; some were unforgettable for other reasons.

In the same classroom, the lecture for the day was discussing human reproductive parts for both the male and female. The professor had just finished showing the anatomy of the female parts on the chalkboard. When it came time for the male body parts, he said, "Now here are the testicles, here the spermatic cord, and here is the glans penis, pointing to the top crown of the penis." When he said it, it sounded like Glen's Penis, and everyone in class turned around and stared at me. I just shook my head to say and sank deep into my seat. I was so embarrassed that you could not tell the color of a tomato from my face. Other instructors left their mark with humor and grit. I will never forget that experience.

My favorite classes were the ones where you could dissect things, like a frog and everything else that they would bring into the classroom. Because I was fascinated with anatomy and the human body, I expressed this to my advisor, who invited me to stay another year at the two-year college so I could enroll in his gross anatomy class that was reserved for only a few students. This would give me an opportunity that very few students get. I could get some other classes out of the way, so when I did make it into a university, I would not have to worry about English and Inorganic Chemistry. I would even get some of my math classes out of the way.

I loved taking math from this teacher who coached football. He had a saying when you're faced with an adversity, tell yourself, "It's just another way to excel when you are going through the difficulty." He also had another saying, "I remember when men were men, and the women were proud of it." He had a way of making math fun.

With confidence growing, I chose to stay another year for this rare opportunity.

The Power of a Promise

Commitments to friends also set a course I didn't fully grasp at the time. Corona was gifted in school; he knew physics and math very well; the two subjects not taught in the study skills lab. These are subjects I needed help with, so Corona came to my rescue.

As we were walking through the hallways of the library after we were done studying, I turned to him and said, "One day, after I graduate from medical school, I will go and treat your family and people in Tonga." He reached out his hand, the same hand that delivered footballs to the quarterback after each huddle, and with the strength of his handshake bound my promise, and said as he looked at me, "I know you will graduate from medical school." He ended up getting a scholarship to Kansas State to play football. I stayed at Ricks College so I could finish up as many of the undergraduate classes before heading off to a big university that I was still trying to find. I did not know the power of a promise, but the promise I made to Corona charted the rest of my academic life. It took me 11 years before I boarded a plane to go to Tonga.

I accomplished another milestone; I finished another year of schooling, passing all my classes, and I am halfway to graduating with my bachelor's degree.

Reflection

From stumbling through early setbacks and low test scores to finding purpose in service, study, and steady character, this journey shows that growth is built on persistence, humility, and hope. I learned to accept imperfect starts, to outwork my weaknesses, and to seek mentors who see the person I can become. I discovered that faith and small daily habits—showing up, studying twice as long, praying for protection, keeping promises, forgiving others, and choosing integrity when no one is watching—create quiet miracles.

Friendship and service widened my world; curiosity in a cadaver lab narrowed my calling; sacrifice and honest work paid for the dream; and every closed door became motivation to try another key. Life's messes, pranks, late nights, and hard classes taught me to laugh, to learn, and to lead with gratitude. If you're facing doubt, let it sharpen your resolve; if you're unsure, explore until conviction clicks; if the road is long, make each mile count.

Time will pass—will you?

Step forward with courage, curiosity, and compassion, and let your consistent effort turn adversity into a life of purpose and impact.

CHAPTER 4

The Storm Before the Calm

*If you want to be the best, you have to do things
that other people aren't willing to do.*

– Michael Phelps

Third Year, Rick's College: Welcome to Gross Anatomy

The main reason I stayed at Ricks College another year was to take an Advanced Gross Anatomy course. I was asked to dissect the entire human body's nervous system from the brain to the toes. It was a year-long project. I was also able to get some of the advanced chemistry and math classes out of the way, along with my English classes, in which I struggle. Corona went off to play football at Kansas State. I got new roommates, but still roomed with my Catholic friend from Wisconsin. We had a mutual agreement that I would attend his church if he came with me to mine. That extra year opened doors to hands-on learning most undergrads have ever seen. That choice soon centered my days around one course that would change everything.

One of the benefits of staying an extra year at Rick's College was the chance to take some advanced courses that I would not get in a university. This course was for the entire year. The college had a cadaver lab where students got to observe and even dissect. Dr Hibbert was the advisor for the class; he saw that I had an interest in anatomy. He offered me a special project. "I want you to dissect the entire nervous system from head to toe," he asked. He was very impressed with my dissecting skills. I was the only one who had a project working on the cadaver for the entire year. I had complete silence and would eagerly go to the lab and dissect, discovering body parts that you could only see in textbooks. Going from the cow heart from the 6th grade table to castrating piglets on the farm, to now working on a human body, was a huge and major accomplishment. As I worked, the body revealed its intricacies—and deepened my sense of purpose. With each new region, my focus sharpened, and my curiosity found a home.

As I made my way from the head through the abdomen and finally into the foot, I was blown away at the complex structures of the foot, all the bones, ligaments, and tendons, all the blood vessels, muscles, and the nervous system. The connection from the brain to the spinal cord was so fascinating to me, I even discovered this person had cancer in her spinal cord.

The fascination sparked in the cadaver lab began to narrow my path toward a specific calling. Naturally, the work at the foot pointed me toward a field where that knowledge mattered every day.

My Quest to Become a Podiatric Surgeon and Physician

A podiatrist is a medical doctor specializing in the diagnosis and treatment of conditions affecting the foot, ankle, and lower leg. They are known as Doctor of Podiatric Medicine (DPM). They are qualified to treat issues ranging from ingrown toenails and bunions to fractures, sports injuries, and diabetic foot problems. Podiatrists can prescribe medication, order X-rays and other tests, perform surgery, and fit custom-made orthotics[1].

When all my dissecting ended at the foot, I was more interested than ever. I was curious to see the ankle joint and to find the location where I broke my ankle in the eighth grade. I was

---

[1] American Podiatric Medical Association. (n.d.). *What is a podiatrist?* American Podiatric Medical Association. Retrieved October 22, 2025, from https://www.apma.org/patients-and-the-public/what-is-a-podiatrist/

so excited to show Dr Hibbert my dissection. He asked, "Have you ever considered Podiatry as a Medical Option?" I had no idea what it was. He explained that they specialize in the foot and ankle and asked me to explore this medical field. With that nudge, I began testing specialties to see what truly fits. To compare paths honestly, I started by checking the option I once imagined for myself.

My quest for finding the cure for asthma has now shifted to Podiatry. I had gone and visited an Allergist and Asthma Doctor in Idaho Falls. I had called the office and decided to shadow the doctor for a few hours. I spent more time in the sterile waiting room than I did with the doctor. I asked him a few questions and observed him working with a few patients. After leaving his office, I knew this was not the specialty for me. The contrast became clear after shadowing a podiatrist who loved what he did. That clarity pushed me to see podiatry up close, where the work matched my interests.

After making a few calls to some podiatrists in Utah, I drove down to their office. My sister had foot surgery by one of them, so this was my foot in the door. Dr. Jex was very nice, pleasant, and so welcoming. He explained, "Do you know what I love about my profession? You get to work on kids, adults, take X-rays, write prescriptions, do surgery, work on the skin, the bones, the muscles, and the nervous system. When a patient comes in, they are in pain, and when they leave, they are smiling." The selling point for me was when he said, "It is the best medical profession for a family lifestyle."

I knew one day I would marry and have kids. The idea of attending my children's sporting events and activities got me more excited than ever. When I got back to school, I went to tell Dr Hibbert this was what I wanted to do. He started to help me in the process. One of the things I had to do was get into a university so I could finish my bachelor's degree. After close to three years of college, I finally knew what I wanted to do in the medical field. To move forward, I had to face a place that once doubted me and laughed at me, and said I could never step foot onto their campus with that ACT score. Knowing the destination made the next academic leap both obvious and intimidating.

You Will Never Set Foot on Our Campus

I knew if I wanted to get into medical school, I had to get into a university, so my advisor recommended that I look at Brigham Young University. The same school laughed at me with my ACT score. When I got my acceptance letter into BYU, the very first thing I wanted to do was search out the recruiter who laughed at me and told me I would never step foot on their campus. Still, I held back my emotions and was very excited to be attending university. I knew I was one step closer to my goal of becoming a surgeon in Podiatry.

After three years at Rick's College, I earned an associate degree in pre-med. I chose not to walk at my graduation because I was not done with school. I watched from a distance as the graduates filed into their seats to receive their diplomas, then I left. I was accepted into BYU, the same school that laughed at me for my ACT score of 7. A feat that even today would be classified as a miracle. To further solidify my path, a scouting trip to a podiatric medical school felt essential.

Road Trip with Corona: Are My Hubcaps Still on My Car?

With Corona having a little time off from football and me having a little time before firefighting, I asked him if he wanted to go on a road trip to California. I had asked the California College of Podiatric Medicine if I could tour the campus, and they gladly told me to come out. I figured if I could put a face with my application, I would have a better chance at getting into their school.

Corona was excited to drive and said that we could stay with his relatives in Sacramento; he had never met them. It was in a very, very bad neighborhood. I did not sleep much that night, not because of the campus tour the next day but because I did not know if I would have a car still parked on the street the next morning. Corona did not seem to be phased, but he did admit that it was indeed a bad neighborhood, and maybe it wasn't such a good idea to visit. After the fact, we then got in the car and made our way to San Francisco. We made it to the medical school. I accomplished what I set out to do as I walked the campus and showed interest in the school. It reconfirmed to me that I was headed into the right profession.

With that reassurance in my pocket, I turned back to campus life—bigger, busier, and far less forgiving.

BYU: Not so Holy of an Experience

Stepping onto BYU's grounds, I immediately felt the shift from small-college familiarity to big-university pace. BYU was a lot larger than the small campus that I previously attended. My professors couldn't care less if you went to class or not. The educational pursuit was more competitive; all my classes were on the bell curve. So, as with many A's in the class, there also had to be the same number of F's. I declared my major as Zoology with a minor in Chemistry. I outlined all the required classes I needed for podiatric medical school before I graduated. I worked closely with an advisor and was assured that if I passed all my classes, I would graduate. Now it was up to me to show them that I, too, belonged here. I did my best to maintain a positive attitude as it did not take long for me to understand life is a boomerang, what you project out comes right back to you. Housing, however, brought its own lesson in endurance.

I had a place arranged to live to go to school, and every student who attended BYU had to have their housing approved by a governing board. Not having much time to find a place, I found a basement apartment, where there were ten students in a three-bedroom and two-bath apartment with one refrigerator. The rule book for the living arrangements was larger than the dress code at the university. Some of the rules were no girls in the apartment, no TV, no music; it was literally a prison. I only used the place for sleeping. I was either on campus studying or at Utah State on the weekend with my brothers.

If the rules were tight, my small acts of individuality were tighter—and sometimes provocative.

My Catholic roommate from Ricks College gave me a Notre Dame baseball cap, which I wore all the time on campus. Boy, talk about death threats from the other students wearing a Catholic hat at a Mormon school was either very daring or stupid. One day, I walked past the head football coach, LaVell Edwards, with my baseball cap. Obviously, I survived the experience because I am here writing about it.

Campus life had its clashes, but the most painful hit came on the field.

I Thought This Was Flag Football: A Personal Experience with a Plastic Surgeon

What started as a casual game turned into an unexpected detour to the ER. Some of my friends talked me into playing intermural flag football. You would think I was either playing rugby or tackling football. On October 17th, 1992, I had an intramural flag football game at 10:00 a.m., and at 10:20 a.m., I was in the emergency room. I went up for a catch, and out of nowhere, I was tackled. When I got up, there was blood all over my face, and everyone was motioning to get medical attention. I did not realize my upper lip had a big opening exposing my teeth. I was rushed into the ER, and the doctor would not touch it and had to call in a plastic surgeon. I had sutures on the inside and outside; the outside was sutured without anesthesia, and I felt every needle stitch.

Healing took time—and I looked for ways to turn downtime into preparation.

Working on My Dexterity for Surgery

I wanted to do something to work on my dexterity, and I wanted to do something that would help my hand-eye coordination for surgery. Because all my classes in school took up most of my day, I resorted to taking private oil painting lessons in the evening. In a way, it was my escape from school and the apartment, and I got to show myself that I could paint no matter what my high school art teacher said. Still, the grind wore me down, and doubts crept in.

I wish I could say school was a cake walk, but there were times I just wanted to go back to bed, pull the sheet over my head, and pretend that nothing ever happened. It got so bad to the point in mid-November that I wanted to drop out of school, but my roommate talked me out of it.

Medical School Interviews: "The Storm Before the Calm"

The whirlwind began before I ever reached the calm. In every storm, there is eventually the calm, but in my case, all the storms happened before the calm. I had sent in my application to the podiatric medical school in San Francisco, hoping for an interview, when I got word that I had been granted an interview. All the noise and distractions around me did not exist. I knew if I could get the interview, I could get into podiatric medical school. I had not even taken the MCAT (Medical College Admission Test) yet, but that did not matter to me; I had my interview.

Arriving early at my interview, the first person I talked with was the admissions officer. Susan happened to be the person who interviewed me. She asked a lot of basic questions about my personal achievements. It really helped me to reduce my anxiety. She asked me questions about the six palms in scouting, to how I liked my visit with Dr Jex when I was at Ricks College.

In the interview, she said it is so great that our school has so many LDS students here. I said yes, it is, "coming from BYU, everyone was LDS except for a few students." She kept saying that it was great having so many applicants and students who are LDS. I nodded my head again in agreement. She repeated the comment. I don't know if she was trying to get me riled up or what, and then she said it is so great to have some many "**L**earning **D**isability **S**tudents" interviewing on our campus. I started laughing, and she asked what was so funny. I explained LDS means Latter Day Saints, not learning disability students. We both laughed.

I had a few other interviews with professors. One of them told me that so many students stress about their grades, but some of the best students are not the ones who get the A's, but the B's in his class. Another professor started by looking over my school records. "I see you having difficulties in physics and chemistry. If I gave you an equation, could you tell me what it is?" I said, "Sorry, I can't." I explained that physics and chemistry were basically a foreign language to me and were very difficult to understand. He admitted to having the same experience.

"I see you have a lot of anatomy experience," he noticed. "You will be more prepared than most students." Even though I did not feel really good about the interviews, I was honest in my answers, and that was the most important thing for me.

With time to spare, I let the city test my convictions in its own quirky way. I finished up with the interviews and had a little time to sightsee, so I took the trolley to Fisherman's Wharf. I was approached by a lady who asked if I would sign a petition to eliminate all cows. I said sure, but let me make a phone call to my father to see what he is going to do with his 150 head of cattle. She was a little disgusted with me and left.

Humor aside, the flight home turned reflective—and resolute.

As I was on the plane flying back, I reflected on my experience. I told myself, if I made it into podiatric medical school, it would be the greatest accomplishment in my schooling. I truly accomplished what most would never even attempt to do after getting a 7 on their ACT. The fate was now in the hands of the committee. All I could do was either stress about it or have faith that all things would work out—I chose the latter. Then came the waiting, and the envelope that could rewrite my future.

The Letter in the Mail: Did I Get In or Didn't I?

The answer arrived quietly, buried in a day that felt ordinary. A few weeks after my interview, I was in my zoology class waiting for my test when a classmate asked me if I had heard back from the Podiatry school. I said I should be hearing back soon. Maybe today or next week. After taking the exam, I did not feel good about my performance, so like clockwork, I went back home, got into bed, and pulled the sheets over my head. I should have checked the mail, as it would have prevented my ritual. The next day, there was a letter on the table. I must have overlooked it. I noticed the letter was from CCPM (California College of Podiatric Medicine).

In a way, it was like getting my mission call; there's a lot of anticipation and apprehension. I took the letter into my room and opened the letter. It said **CONGRATULATIONS** on being accepted. There was so much gratitude in my heart, it did not matter what I had gone through; I was going to medical school!

Always Going by Intuition: A Lesson from My Father

Finishing up the semester, I went home for Christmas, and was sitting in the living room, when out of the blue, my father asked me to move my car off the street. I waited a while, and again he reminded me to move the car off the street. So I got up and moved my car down into the driveway, when out of nowhere, a car that was speeding lost control, crossed lanes, and ended up where I had previously parked the car.

How did my dad know this in advance? Had I not moved it, the car would have been totaled. It is said that prayer is our way of communicating with God, and intuition is God's way of communicating with us. That night, God was speaking to my father. My father and his faith, and his prayers saved me a lot of potential headaches.

That brush with intuition set the tone for a season when plans kept changing—and faith had to fill the gaps.

Sorry, "You're Going to Stay Another Year for One Class"

Midway through my last semester, my health had taken a turn for the worse. I was very congested, and I blamed the steel plant, but it was more than likely my diet and lack of sleep. Heading to the down stretch of my graduating, I took the required MCAT (Medical College Admission Test), had all the remaining classes that needed to be taken and then my advisor called me into the office to inform me that my major had a few changes, He said they added one more class that is needed to be taken before I could graduate, I said, "Ok, how do I get enrolled?" He said the genetics class is only offered in the fall, so see you next year.

It was too late to change my major, and I did not want to stay another semester, let alone another day at BYU. I called up the medical school and informed them of my circumstances. They said the committee would need to meet to discuss the matter, as they required all students to have a bachelor's degree to go to medical school. I continue to work hard in school. A few weeks later, I got word back from the school that they said the committee made an exception, finish up everything, and come on out: "See you in the Fall."

I never did graduate from BYU; I tell people I went from being an ASS (**ass**ociate degree), skipping the BS (Bull S***) Bachelor of Science, and got my Doctorate. I am disappointed that I never finished my bachelor's degree. The idea of going to medical school allowed me to be more excited than not finishing what

I originally set out to do, "graduate from a university." Maybe it was the school's intention not to graduate a student who got a 7 on their ACT. They may have got the last laugh, but when they call me up asking for donations from the alumni, I say, "I never graduated; sorry, no money from me."

With acceptance secured, I tried to savor a last bit of freedom—one more outing before the real grind began.

Fishing Trip Before Med School: The Object Is Larger Than It Appears

Have you ever paid attention to the saying that the object in the mirror is closer than it appears in your vehicle's mirror? I learned the hard way, and I wasn't even near a vehicle. Trying to get a fishing trip in before I ventured off to medical school, I went with my two brothers up in the local canyon. I was wearing sandals, and my brothers had their shoes on. I crossed the creek first and then looked back, only to notice my two brothers trying to figure out how to get across the creek without getting their shoes wet. The good brother that I was, I went back. I found a rock in the water that appeared to be the right size. I lifted them out of the water and placed them on two other rocks so they could use them to step on and over the water. I did not realize the water made the rocks appear smaller than they were. As I went to pick up this rock, I had immediate shooting pain go down my leg. I am only telling you this story because this one incident had a major impact on my life. That sudden pain followed me to San Francisco, shadowing the excitement of a brand-new start.

First Year of Medical School 1993-94

Prior to leaving for medical school, my mom prepared a wonderful dinner, and my dad gave me one of his father's blessings. He blessed me with a clear mind and good study habits. A good friend of mine drove me to Orem, where I was going to catch a ride out to San Francisco with a family that was also going to the same school. We decided to share rent as it was very expensive to live in the city. We left at 8:10 p.m. and arrived at 7:30 the next morning. The apartment was on Pacific Ave, right in the heart of San Francisco. I unpacked my things, lay out a blanket, and fell asleep. The move was real—and so were the aches and adjustments of settling into a new city.

It has now been a week, and my bed finally arrived. I had been sleeping on the floor with blankets, and my back did not like it. I bought a dresser from a thrift store for my clothes. I often went to the parks in the city to observe and clear my mind. I soon learned which parks were safe and which to stay away from. The ones with the families and dogs are the ones I visited the most. I feel like I am living a dream being here. I keep rubbing my eyes, and the irritation that I am causing tells me it is a reality.

The Friday before the start of school was orientation day. It was good to meet all my classmates; everyone had a name tag that listed their names and the university where they graduated. I noticed Universities like UCLA, Stanford, BYU, UC Berkeley, Utah, Oklahoma, Michigan, Colorado, and so many others. My name tag said Ricks College. It was the only name tag with a college and not a university. Nobody knew that I did not have my Bachelor of Science degree, with the exception of the school admissions office. I just did my best to blend in with the rest of my classmates.

Then the firehose opened, and the routine turned relentless.

Drinking from a Fire Hydrant: "My First Week"

I quickly started to see the student packs developing. Everyone was joining study groups to help them get the best grades possible. I was in a group that had three other students. The classes consisted of General Anatomy, my favorite, and then there were Physiology, Biochemistry, Lower Extremities, and Histology. The word was that for every one hour in class, you needed two hours of study. This meant no sleep; my study group would study late at night, only to sleep a few hours and then start over again. We even studied on the way to the school picnic on Saturday until we were in a car accident, when the driver of the group was not paying attention to the car in front of him. That did not help my back. I ended up sitting on the right side of the classroom the rest of the school year so I could stretch out my left leg, which I had been experiencing shooting pain in.

Life outside the classroom offered its own jolts—a different kind of education.

One interesting thing I saw in the grocery store was a tall black man wearing a dress who passed by me in the aisle started to argue with a Hispanic man. The Hispanic man grabbed a broom, and the black man pulled out a switchblade. Luckily, security came and broke it up. Shopping at the grocery stores in San Francisco is way different from the one I worked at back home.

Amid the chaos, week two brought small roles, bigger responsibilities, and mounting pain.

During my second week, I got up at 6 a.m., went to school, met more classmates, was elected to be the class representative, and experienced my first day in gross anatomy. The pain in my back makes it harder for me to sit and study. It seems I am in school all day, then I go back home for a short bite to eat, and then off to study again. Going to bed at 1 or 2 a.m. in the morning, only to get up at 5 a.m. to study again, was something I had not experienced. I purchased a bike to help with travel time so I could study more.

The academic pressure soon spilled into my support system.

You Have One Week to Leave

The group approached me and told me they did not want me in their study group anymore. They wanted me out by the end of the week. They still wanted me to be in the gross anatomy lab group, as that was my strength. I did not fight it and just started studying on my own. When I was told to leave the group, I made the choice also to leave the Anatomy lab.

They were not happy when I told them I was leaving the gross anatomy lab group, but I was not too happy being told to leave the study group either. I finally found another group that welcomed me into their anatomy group. What made matters even worse was being told to find a new place to live, and I had a week to do it. I was sharing rent with one of the members of the study group. With only five weeks into the school year, I was now looking for a place to live on top of trying to keep up with the schoolwork and taking exams that were killing me. Tests were always on Monday for first-year students. And every Monday, it was a different class to be tested. Luckily, one of my good classmates offered his laundry room floor to crash, which was out of the city, and took several hours of traveling each day to school and back. Even the daily commute became a test—a reminder of how thin the margin had become.

One day, because of an accident on the freeway, it took us two and half hours to get to school. We tried to find ways to get around the accident, but we ended up in a bad part of Oakland. When a homeless man has a baseball bat in his shopping cart, you know you're in a bad neighborhood.

Reflection

From the first spark in a quiet cadaver lab to the long nights of study, setbacks, and small miracles that followed, this journey proves that purpose grows where curiosity, grit, and faith meet. I learned that doors open when you show up with honest effort and humble confidence; that intuition—often carried by those who love us—can redirect us just in time; that rejection, detours, and even pain can refine our aim; and that service-centered work gives trials their meaning. When rules feel rigid, keep your individuality; when fear rises, choose humor; when discouragement hits, lean on good people and keep moving.

Be transparent about your weaknesses, double down on your strengths, and let persistence outwork perfection. Approach life like a surgeon and an artist: steady hands, patient eyes, and a heart set on healing. Trust that faith beats fear, that resilience compounds over time, and that every step—whether on campus, in a lab, or through a hard neighborhood—can lead you closer to the calling only you can fulfill.

CHAPTER 5

Sleeping at the Bus Stop

I have been driven many times upon my knees.
By the overwhelming conviction that I had
nowhere else to go

– Abraham Lincoln

What It's Like Sleeping at a Bus Stop

The first night that I slept at the bus station to go to school was a small glimpse of what the homeless people go through. Luckily, I only had to do this for a few nights. I finally got a lead on a place to move back to the city; the only downside was that it was sandwiched between two government projects that created some very scary times to walk through.

One day, while walking through the projects, a homeless man approached me and asked for a quarter. I said to him, "Sir, I wish I could give you something, but my schooling is going to cost me over two hundred thousand by the time I am done, and I need every dime in my pocket." He then reached into his pocket, pulled out a dollar bill, and said: "Here, let me help you!"

Your ID That Everyone Wanted to Know

I soon learned that school was so competitive, being the top student in the class meant getting the top residency program. Some students would hide the material in the library that was used for a particular test, then, after the test, the material would somehow show up again.

Getting an upper edge on other students was the consensus among some of the students. Every class would post their test result outside the professor's door the next day after the exam. Everyone rushed to see their score and then rushed off to study again for the next test. Because someone was looking over my shoulder every time I went to view my test results, I moved my finger down the top, stopping at a few names. Still, my eyes were at the bottom looking up to see if I was at the bottom. Just like I did when I went to see if I made the basketball team in high school, I never let anyone know my number or class ranking. But only a few students knew I was struggling to pass my classes.

On November 7th, 1993, my journal states:

I got my first F on an examination here at CCPM. I still get up early to study, even though I do not have a study group currently. I seem to retain things more in the morning than at night when I am exhausted and ready for sleep. I am starting to study with other classmates, most of them are very helpful and offer to help me with some of the classes. I still really don't know what I did to the members of my first study group, but what is done is done, and I have to move on.

Deep Gratitude for Doug, My Classmate

Just when the grind felt heaviest, help arrived with a different rhythm and a kinder pace. I owe deep gratitude and appreciation to Doug. He lived in the same complex but in a different building. He noticed somehow that I was struggling, so he invited me to study with his group.

Being a little startled by the last group, I was hesitant, but he said, "Look, this will be different." He had breaks in studying and would exercise and really utilized his time well, but in a more relaxed way. Doug insisted that I go to the 49ers football game against the New Orleans Saints. I had never been to such an event; the fans were crazy and funny, and I spent more time observing the fans while trying to pay attention to the game. For some odd reason, getting out and relaxing was more beneficial to my studies than studying nonstop all night with very few to no breaks. His method was working. With a steadier cadence, even the small routines started to matter.

For lunch, we would walk over to Taco Bell and get the one-dollar tacos and then head back to school for studying or classes. Doug liked going to class like I did, while most of the more competitive students stayed home studying for the upcoming tests. Every lecture was recorded on a cassette tape, and each student was assigned to write out the recorded lecture and make a copy for every student. I still preferred to be in class over relying on the dictated lectures. Balance didn't just live in classrooms and libraries—it showed up on weekends too.

On the weekends, a lot of my classmates would get together at various student apartments in the evenings. I was always invited to be their designated driver. I was approached many times at these parties and offered a beer. It only took one time to say no, thank you. By then, when someone would come up to me and offer me a beer, they would say, "No, Glen does not drink." They had great respect for me because of that. They always would tell me that I was different from the other twenty-one LDS students who never would go to these class parties.

The Happiest Grade I Ever Got in School

When the semester finally came to a close, the results told their own story. December 16th, 1993: I am in the Oakland Airport flying back to Utah to spend Christmas with my family. I am catching up in my journal writing: I started with a C in General Anatomy and Histology, but ended up with a B. In Biochemistry, I was at a C and dropped to a D. I missed a C by one percent. I felt crushed and wanted to go back to bed and pull the sheet over my head like I did in undergrad, but I remember what my mother told me: "Get out of bed, and face your defeat."

Don't let this one thing define you. The one class, "Physiology," I feared the most about failing, I found out I got a D. That was the happiest D I ever got. I passed all my classes and did not have to repeat a class. This was the most trying and difficult semester of my schooling.

Second Semester: A Bill Murray Groundhog Day Experience

Still fresh in my mind of what last semester was like, I now had to face the same classes for Part Two. I am thankful I have a roof over my head, but it too came with some challenges; not only did I live between two government projects, but my living items were very sparse. I had a chair, but no table, a futon for my couch/bed, and a few hangers to hang my clothes on, and that was about it. One day, while I stopped by the apartment, I must have been followed. I noticed a letter slipped under my door. Inside the letter was a full naked guy on it that said: "I want you." I had gay professors and gay friends, but being hit on was a very different experience for me, coming from a small town with Christian beliefs, plus I like girls.

One way I found to help reduce the cost-of-living expenses is to take a new prospective student and show them around campus. The bonus was that the school paid for my lunch, no more one-dollar tacos at Taco Bell. One day, I tried out the political scene and went with a few of my classmates to the state capital building in Sacramento. It was our goal to educate the assemblymen about Podiatry. One of the assemblymen said that prisons and education were higher priorities than health and medicine. I find it interesting how he put prisons and schools together.

As school continued to provide those great lessons of life. I continued to do everything I could to pass my classes. I met with my Biochemistry and Physiology professors weekly, along with repeating this poem my mom sent me:

Don't Quit
When things go wrong, as they sometimes will
When the road you're trudging seems all uphill
When the funds are low and the debts are high,
and you want to smile, but you have to sigh,
when care is pressing you down,
Rest if you must, but don't you quit.
Success is failure turned inside out,
the silver tint of the clouds of doubt,
And you can tell how close you are.
It may be near when it seems distant,
So, stick to the fight when you're hardest hit;
It's when things go wrong that you mustn't quit.

Visiting the Homeless Shelter to the Surgery in the Clinic: A First for Everything

My first experience in a clinical setting, I was paired up with a third-year student, a doctor, and a few classmates at a homeless shelter. We worked the patient up, taking a history and presenting it back to the third-year student and doctor. We worked on several patients. It was neat, taking a patient from start to finish with what we had available. I notice homeless people did appreciate our services. There was a lot of drug and alcohol addiction, poor hygiene, and bad shoes, lack of socks, and people who really needed foot care.

Soon, the learning curve sharpened—from shelter exams to the bright lights of a procedure room.

One day, I was walking down the hallway, and a fourth-year student invited me: "Do you want to do a surgery?" Hello yes! I would love to! First-year students were not seen in the school clinic, and even assisting in surgery was not permitted. I followed the fourth year in the clinic. He told me that we are going to remove an ingrown toenail. Then he said, "What I need you to do is fill up this syringe with some lidocaine, then I want you to numb up the toe, and then remove the ingrown toenail. Are you ready?" I nodded my head, but my insides were saying, "Hold on."

I went into the room where the patient was waiting. The fourth-year student showed me how to inject. I started to feel a little woozy, but I got the toe numb, then he asked me to take the ingrown out. He showed me where to cut the nail, and I did it. By then, my stomach was really woozy. He asked me to bandage the toe. I was really feeling like I was going to pass out, so I elevated the chair a little and told the patient that this was protocol to help with the bleeding. I held on to the edge of the chair. I would lift my head, every once in a while, to ask the patient if they were ok. Finally, the fourth year came in and asked how everything was. I said everything's great, then I went into the other room and lay on the floor and took a deep breath, trying not to pass out.

All it took was this one experience, and it fixed my sour stomach of being in surgery. This was way different from when I observed my primary doctor back home. When he asked if I wanted to observe a surgery case to see if I wanted to go into medicine, I was only observing; here, I was the one doing the procedure.

Get up and Go to School: That Is What My Gut Told Me

March 22nd, 1994: Still getting up real early to study, but too nervous to walk through the projects so early in the morning to go to school, I resorted to staying at my place and studying. This morning was different. I felt impressed to leave and go to school. At first, I fought it, but it was too strong, so I acted on that feeling.

While I was in the elevator, a friendly old man commented, "Boy, it's too early. Where are you going so early?" I responded, "Just going to school."

"What school do you go to?"

"The Podiatry school is just down the street."

"Oh, you're a doctor?" I said, "No, just a student, but one day I will."

He started describing his ailments to me about his feet. As the door opened to the elevator, there was a lady with a small child. She was frantically screaming for help: "Please help me, my son is choking."

The boy had his hands around his neck and was gasping for air. The man who was with me said, "This fellow is a doctor; he can help you." I had no experience treating anyone who was choking. I went over to the boy and helped him dislodge the object that was stuck in his throat. He started to breathe normally again. The mother and the young boy were very happy. I made my way to school like nothing had happened.

Was I becoming like my father and having those gut feelings and intuition before an event happened? Even with small victories, the streets could turn in an instant.

"If You Look Back, I Will Kill You"

April 29th, 1993: I remember one day, while walking back to the apartment, it was on the day that Rodney King was beaten in Los Angeles. I was unaware of what was going on as I did not watch TV or listen to the radio. A person with a deep voice came up from behind me and said, "Do not look back or I will kill you!" He told me, "Keep walking, you piece of white trash." I never looked back, so I don't know if he had a knife or a gun, but I survived another day to write about it.

Printed Diploma from the Computer in the School Library

Aside from Doug's help throughout the year, I made friends with a very good classmate, Chris. He, too, had difficulties of his own trying to survive school. He had to work to pay for his schooling and rent, as he was not a US citizen at the time. If he were in school, he would have been fine, but he had to pay for his schooling and could not take out any loans. Last week of school, we went to the library, and he printed out a diploma with our names on it. Mine said Dr Glen N Robison. I kept that diploma paper and tacked it to the wall to see it every day.

We finished up school, and I went back home for my last year of fighting fires. I figured I needed to get out in nature again, and with the few months off, I took advantage of this. Chris stayed back and continued to work. The money I made, I gave to Chris so he could pay for the portion that he needed to enroll in school.

Do You Know What D Stands for?

June 9th, 1994: I passed all my classes. As I was traveling back home for the summer, I caught a ride with a good friend, Jared. He was one of the students who had a good heart and knew my situation with my academics. He said something to me, "Glen, do you know what D stands for? D stands for Doctor."

When you get that doctorate, I don't think you will ever be asked what you got in Biochemistry or Physiology. Yes, I did get a few D's in my first year, but thanks to Chris, Doug, Jared, and a few others, I pulled my grades up from a failing grade, and I passed my first year. With that perspective ringing in my ears, I stepped into year two, aiming for consistency over perfection.

Staying Persistent: Second Year 1994-95

Aug 28th, 1994: I am back in San Francisco. I was told this would be one of the easiest semesters. Boy, were they wrong. I have moved out of the apartments by the projects and moved further out into the Sunset district. It requires me to either take the bus to school or drive to school with limited parking. If I had known what was going to happen to me this year, I may have stayed back home and taken up fighting fires as a full-time job.

New places and new routines opened unexpected doors. Dr Richardson stopped me in the hallway and asked if I would help tutor General Anatomy. He had some students who needed some help. I have five students with plans on adding three more. I really enjoy it. Doug continues to be a lifesaver; we still study together even though we live in completely different places.

Was I a Student with Learning Disabilities (and I Don't Mean LDS)

Still trying to figure out how I could improve my grades, I agreed to meet with some medical residents in Psychology. The first person I met asked me a bunch of questions to see if I had any learning disabilities like Dyslexia. What they found was that I learned by visual memory, and I memorized everything from what I read, as I could recall which page in the book the subject was located on. When they told me in medical school that you can only memorize what is on the test, the Psychology resident said he would like to do more tests on me, but another student would be doing these. Thinking there was more guidance to help in my schoolwork, I gladly accepted. Once I applied the principles, I got my first 4.0 in school.

Gains in the classroom were encouraging, but the biggest hurdle still waited at the end of year two.

National Board Part I: The Highest Peak I Had to Climb

In medical school, you are required to take two national boards: Part I, at the end of the second year, is all academics, physiology, biochemistry, pharmacology, general anatomy, and all the basic sciences, and Part II, you take right before graduation, where a majority of its content is clinical.

To pass the exam, you had to pass each subject with 75 percent or greater. There was no averaging out. This meant if you got a 74 percent in just one subject and 90 percent in all the other subjects, you still failed the boards. Taking the boards was stressful enough, but when I got my test results back, I had failed. One subject, I got a 74 percent; all the other ones I passed. This required me to retake the test the following school year, as they only offered it once a year. I never let anyone in my class know of my failing the boards, not even my closest friends. What I will tell you is that I ended up taking this test five times. I kept failing a subject that I had passed in previous attempts. I kept getting a 74 percent in one subject.

The Halfway Point: Does It Get Any Better?

Third year of Medical School: The stress of this past year, with failing the national board's part I, the sleepless nights of worrying if I pass my classes or not, and then the physical ailments of the bulged disc in my lower back, was all coming to a point in my body. I stayed away from the school politics and volunteering and just devoted my time to studying. It was so nice being over the basic science in the classroom setting, but I still had to keep studying it to pass my boards Part I.

Draft Day: All About Placement for a Good Externship

The beginning of the third year was the year to prepare for what externships you would be doing in your fourth year. It was the one chance to land a good residence program. Much emphasis was placed on the big surgical programs in Atlanta and in Washington. Not only were you competing for an externship with your classmates, but you were also competing against all the other schools in the country and their students. The key was to get a good draft pick when all the students would meet to pick their programs. The best months to do the externships were August, September, or October for the program that you wanted to do your residency program. By this time, the interviews were starting, and having your presence seen and felt in these teaching institutes gave you a foot in the door. You could still interview for a program without doing an externship. Still, it was more favorable for you to get one so the directors could see you.

One of those externships that really caught my eye was in South Dakota at the Veterans Hospital, but they only offered the program to students from schools in the Midwest and the East Coast. I wrote a letter to the director asking if he would consider opening a slot for a California student. I guess I will have to wait until the end of this year to find out if they will open a slot and if I can get a good draft pick.

Giving Birth to a One-Gram Stone with Thorns

One evening after studying for one of my classes, I was having this pain in my back that would not go away. It was a different pain than I had ever felt before. When I started to pee blood, I was going over in my mind every class lecture that I had sat in, trying to figure out what my diagnosis was. I knew living on Costco muffins, root beer floats, and the one-dollar tacos from Taco Bell and along with the stresses of school, was the cause.

Because the pain was so intense, I had my roommate drive me to the emergency room. I literally crawled there, so they took me in and asked me some questions. When they realized I was a legitimate patient and not seeking pain medications, they gave me a shot of some good stuff that took the pain away, but only for a short time. They told me that I had developed a kidney stone and had to pee in this strainer for the next few days and follow up with a urologist.

After a few days of intense pain controlled by Percocet, I gave birth to this gram of stone that looked like Grape Nuts cereal, spikes and all. I followed up with the urologist, and they ordered me a CT scan to see if there were more stones. They injected contrast dye into my arm to see if there were any remaining kidney stones, and none were found.

All I was told to do was drink water—no mention of changing my diet or stress. I ended up passing eight stones. I continued my Costco muffins, root beer floats, and one-dollar tacos. I wish I could say this was the last time for this health issue, but it was only the beginning.

My Dream Job: Back in the Gross Anatomy Lab, Dissecting at Night

Now that all the basic science classes were over, and I never had to take another biochemistry or physiology exam, I could focus more on the clinical classes such as biomechanics, radiology, emergency medicine and general medicine, and surgery. These subjects were more practical, and usually, I could reason out the test questions to the correct answer in a timely manner.

Dr Richardson approached me in the hallway and thanked me for tutoring the underclassmen, then offered me another job that paid. He offered me to be a prosecutor for Gross Anatomy, I immediately accepted and was told to drop by his office to get the keys to the lab. This motivated me to get my studies in other classes so I could spend time in the lab.

Nights were the best time to dissect, as there was nobody there to bother me. The school was open because of the small hospital that was part of the school campus. The nights I would work in the lab, I would drive my vehicle, no longer worrying about walking through the projects. I remember one night, I had my hammer and chisel; I was chipping away some bone, and then suddenly, I hit the chisel on the table and heard this loud metal sound. I apologized to the cadaver and continued dissecting. I always respect the dead and was appreciative that they gave me the opportunity to learn anatomy on their body they donated.

I followed the manual very closely on each project and tagged the important structure for the student to learn from. But working on the back was more difficult than what the manual described. I decided to go around the manual and do it my way; it was as if I were performing surgery on the back. When I exposed all the nerve endings, with the dorsal and ventral rami, all the foramina, and without any damage, I showed my professor, and he said, "You should talk with the Neurology professor; she would be very interested in what you are doing."

When I showed her my project, she asked me if I'd be interested in writing this up so we can put it in the library. I did my step-by-step approach and took photos, and gave it to her. In a way, it was my first publication. It was used in the medical school library for other students to reference when doing the dissection of the spinal cord.

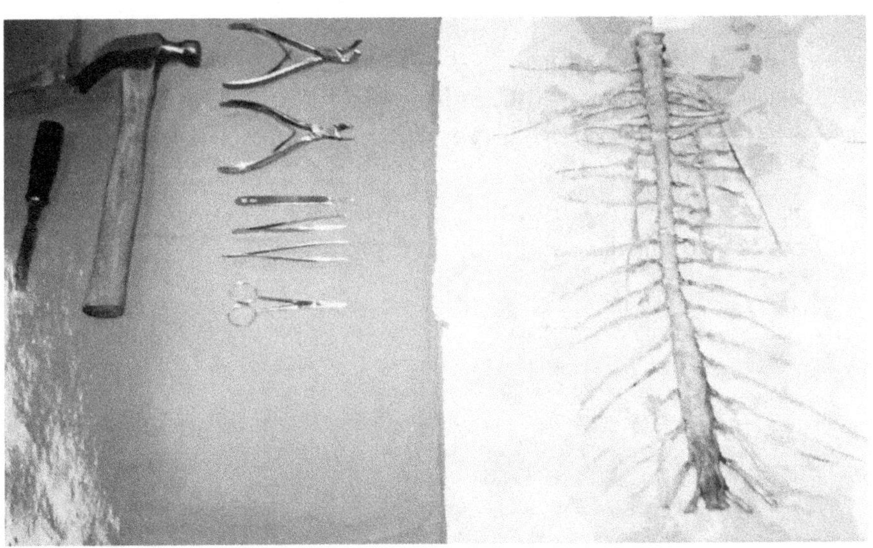

Human spinal cord with the tool used to dissect.

Reflection

Across long nights at bus stops, tight budgets, dangerous streets, hard classes, failed boards, kidney stones, and the pressure of externships, the throughline was simple: keep showing up, keep learning, and keep serving. The grades mattered, but grit mattered more. The D that stood for "Doctor"; the finger tracing the list while the eyes searched upward, and the fifth try at the boards all testified that progress is often persistence in disguise. I learned that help comes when you both ask and offer—Doug's steady friendship, Chris's makeshift diploma and shared sacrifice, Jared's perspective, the classmates I tutored, the patients at the shelter, and the child in the elevator taught me that we lift best when we lift together.

I learned to adapt—study in the mornings, learn my own wiring, take breaks, move my body, and turn curiosity into contribution—until the lab became a place where reverence met discovery. Most of all, I learned to trust the quiet nudge to act, to find humor and gratitude in lean seasons, and to measure myself by courage, kindness, and consistency rather than by rank.

When life tightens, simplify; when fear whispers, step forward; when you fall short, reframe, refine, and try again. Approach each day as a new rep: show up, serve someone, learn one thing, protect your health, and take the next honest step. Over time, those small, stubborn steps turn survival into purpose and setbacks into the very stairs you climb.

CHAPTER 6

From Breath to Death: My Personal Experience

It is not death that a man should fear,
but he should fear never beginning to live.

— Marcus Aurelius

My Brother's Wedding and the Promise I Made to Him

The scriptures always refer to death as "The pains of death." If you really think about it, the only two types of pain that are never spoken about by humans The one being the birth canal because those memories were removed. Ask a child what it was like coming out of the birth canal, and see if they can tell you. The other birth is the one first mentioned; it is not often spoken of by the human being because most do not come back to share it with us. Since I cannot recall my birth experience, I will share with you my death experience. Here is my personal journey to the place that so few get to talk about. This is my own experience and does not reflect on any other person who has had a death experience, but it was as real as your first kiss.

I was so ready to have my spring break from school. My brother called me the night before I was headed back home to confirm I would be at the wedding. He had planned his wedding around my schedule so I could attend. I once again promised him I would be there and hung up the phone. I had my bags packed the night before and was ready to make the 10-hour drive back home. I got up real early the next day and threw my bags in the truck. I had also packed some snacks of Hostess fruit pies, donuts, and Gatorade to eat on the way. I only planned on stopping to fill the vehicle up with gas and purposely did not drink any water because I did not want to stop and take pee breaks on the roadside. The road home was long and quiet, and the plans were simple—until the familiar ache returned.

Visiting My Family Doctor Was Not on My Planned Schedule

I went through all my cassette tapes several times as the middle of Nevada had no radio station signals. I spent a good amount of time in silence as I pondered what I would be asking the Utah Jazz doctor when I got to meet him, also on my trip back home. Exhausted by the drive, I went right to bed when I arrived home, awakened early in the morning with the same pain in my back that landed me in the Emergency room a few months prior, and I knew I had another kidney stone. My father, seeing that I was in pain, told me that I should go and see the family doctor. I made the call to the clinic, and they worked me in for a morning appointment.

A routine visit for a familiar problem sets the stage for something no one expected.

The doctor confirmed that I had a kidney stone from his clinical examination, but wanted me to get a contrast dye study to see if the stone had passed. Little did I know that I was less than an hour away and that it would completely change my life.

I went over to the hospital and met up with the radiologist and his staff. He went through his questions and felt that a contrast dye study would be beneficial to see if I had passed the stone. He did not seem worried at all about giving me another injection of the dye, even with it being only a few months ago back in San Francisco.

The doctor had me lay down on this hard table so my face was looking at him, he then took my arm off the table and with one hand he prepped the skin with alcohol, took out the large 50cc syringe with the needle at the end and broke my skin causing few drops of blood to drop to the floor, he then placed the arm back on the table. He started to push the dye into my body. I find it odd that dye and die are pronounced the same but have completely different meanings, but today they mean the same.

Code Blue, Cold Blue: Indicating the Color of My Face?

The staff person was instructed to take her first film. She did, as she came back to reposition me, and went back to make another film. She glanced back, and I was completely blue. I was trying to scream, "Help me; Please help me." But I could not speak, so all I could do was put my hands around my throat as if to say I am choking. She immediately called for Code Blue to activate the rapid response medical team. Code blue does not mean the color of the person, but it means "Stop what you are doing and get the hell over to the place that code blue was initiated."

There is a medical report that will give their 4 hours of resuscitation account, but here is my personal account of what I saw, heard, felt, and thought during my near-death experience.

As the doctor rushed in to start the medication to stop the rapid heart rate that was now over 200, I could hear everything going on. Still, I could not speak. I was trying to help them by saying, "Get the correct medications into my system." I could hear them say. "Get the epi." I was trying to tell them, "Get the epi 1 to 1000." Still, they were pushing 1 to 10,000, a more diluted epinephrine to help combat the reaction. While trying to speak, I was also trying everything so I could breathe just a normal breath to allow some oxygen back into my blue face.

The Most Peaceful Place I Have Ever Traveled to

As they were pushing more meds into my body to help the heartbeat as it dropped below 40, that was the last time I tried to breathe on my own. I immediately saw these lights that would cause anyone to squint due to the brightness. These bright lights were followed by the most peaceful place that I have ever been to, and still to this day, I have never experienced that kind of peaceful feeling. It was a feeling of complete peace; no worries, no anger, no fear, no trying to do this or trying to do that, but a place where words like blissfulness and joy are used to describe, a place that anyone would die to be there. While I was enjoying this place, a thought came to mind: How is it possible to think when my body is lying there on the table? How is it possible to see what was going on, and how is it possible I could hear everything that was going on?

As I was observing the excitement in the room, the thought of my promise to my brother that I would be there on his wedding came to my mind. So I asked, thinking through a thought, "Could I please go back so I could fulfill the promise I made to my brother?"

At that moment, that place of peace and bright, beautiful, colorful lights now shifted, and I was once again participating in helping the medical team to survive this horrific event. When I was able to squeeze in a breath again, the medical team moved me into the emergency department, where I could be closely monitored.

The medical report said it took them four hours of resuscitation, but to me it felt like five to ten minutes. The first question I asked when I was able to speak again was, "Did someone turn on the lights in the room?" The medical staff told me that no lights were turned on. One of the doctors said to me, "You should not be here; either you have a strong will to live, or you have something great to accomplish, but medically you should not be here."

All I know is I was like a Christmas tree, having multiple strands of IV lines wrapped around my arms. My chest and lungs felt like I had multiple gut punches. It was nice to see with my physical eyes and speak with my two lips again, but it was even nicer to feel the touch of another human hand. It felt so amazing as the doctor placed his hand on mine and said, "I am glad you're back. Your parents should be here soon."

Sounding the Fire Alarm: The Only Way to Find My Dad

So, what else happened while the medical team was helping? I assumed my mother was in the garden, my father was at the farm, and my brother was making preparations for his wedding. I was in a place where I had no worries, not even my next exam or test coming up the following week. I did not even worry about my not passing the National Boards part I; all the troubles of life and the worries of the next day did not exist. It seems the only people in the world who had a care in the world were the medical team below, frantically doing everything they could to help me see another day.

Nobody outside that X-ray room had any idea what I was going through. The medical staff decided to contact my father because they did not know I would make it. They placed several calls to my parents' landline at their home, but no one was home to pick up the phone. There was only one other option, and that was to activate the town's emergency system.

In the small town, there was an alert system for fires, as the fire department was solely managed by volunteers. In order to make people aware of the dangerous fire, they would sound the alarm system, kind of like the ones you would see in Hawaii to alert the people of a tsunami or in the Midwest to alert the people of a tornado. In my town, there were two large sirens placed at each end of the town, and when they went off, everyone could hear them from miles away.

After activating the fire alarms, a message was sent over every scanner in town, and the pagers of every volunteer firefighter relayed a message: "Alison Robison, if you get this message, please get to the hospital as soon as you can." My uncle, who happened to be in the volunteer fire department, got the message on his pager while working down on the farm. He rushed over to another distant field where my father was and told him he had better head to the hospital.

I can only imagine the thoughts that went through my father's mind: "Why do I need to go to the hospital? Did something happen to my boy that I sent to see the family doctor?" As fast as his little blue truck that was held together by baling wire, he went home first before going to the hospital. He took a shower and put on clean clothes, and then headed to the hospital.

This little act of cleaning up before going to the hospital told me his fear was of having to bury another child. I never asked my father why he never came to the hospital directly. But in my mind, this was the only thing that made sense. He also probably went into his little closet, where he felt closest to God, and knelt in prayer and pleaded with him to be able to see his boy alive. Maybe this was around the same time that I had the thought come into my mind to go back to fulfill a promise; I guess I will never know. I wish I had asked my parents more things. If I could say this one thing to anyone who still has a parent, if you have been wanting to ask your parents a question, don't delay asking. You may never get the opportunity again; when you have that urge, just ask them.

Death is real, and the pains of it are also very real. When someone dies, some may experience long durations while others experience the shorter version, but all visit this place that is distantly different from Earth but somehow feels like it is attached.

I used to feel that people fear death because of this pain. But the more I reflect on death, it is not the pain that one fears, but it is the separation of the body and the spirit. The human life that we experience when we touch, taste, and feel things. The spirit loves being wrapped in the skin of our body. It loves the human touch that only exists when we touch an object like a paintbrush or the reins of a horse. It loves the hugs and the kisses of our loved ones. It is the one single thing that keeps everyone here. You could say a spirit would die to have the ability to touch again, but that would not make sense because when the body goes into the dirt or vase, it is gone. Yes, the spirit still thinks, sees, and hears, and everything going on around us, but the spirit would give anything to touch and taste again.

The Doctor Wants You to Take This Anti-Psychotic Medication

I never realized why I had to go through this experience until later in my residency and career. So why did I finally come out and talk about my near-death experience? I feel it was time; this world needs more hope and joy than ever before, and if this can bring a little light and joy to someone, then it is worth going through what I went through.

I also had an experience with the school doctor back in San Francisco, who also taught at the school, but was also the doctor that students would go and see when a medical situation presented that did not need emergency attention. I told him what I went through during my near-death experience. I went into details while sitting in his clinic. When he left the room right after I shared this with him, he returned with a prescription pad and handed me a script for an anti-psychotic medication. I left his clinic and tore the prescription into pieces, tossing the script into the garbage can on my way out of his office. To have someone tell me I was fabricating a story was not worth my time or energy, so I never shared in detail what I experienced for many years.

I ended up making it to my brother's wedding as promised, and I also made it to one of the team doctors for the Utah Jazz.

The Long-awaited Lottery Picks for Externship Draft Day

The long-awaited day was just weeks away to determine our lives as podiatrists. The one day that would define our three previous years of schooling was hanging in the fate of the draft pick for the externship that would land a residency program that everyone was competing for and not just our school, but the entire country of Podiatry schools.

I had heard that the program from South Dakota gave one slot to a California student; this was the first time in their history. The only thing that worried me was that the time slot to go extern with them was in the most prime month, and there was only one slot. I felt like I was competing against all the other students in my class.

On draft day, everyone placed their name in a bucket, and as a name was picked and read, that would be the order for picking our externships for our fourth year. The first name was read, and everyone congratulated the person. Then the next name was read, and the stars must have been aligned as it was my name called out. I did not stick around to hear the other students' placements; I knew I was the second student to choose my programs over a hundred other classmates. I knew my top pick and did not share it with anyone over the next week. Boy, those students who did not have much to do with me were sure friendly to find out if I was picking the top surgical externship that they had their eyes on, with only a few slots available.

After giving us a week or so to research our programs, all the students filed into the same room on draft day. All the externship programs were listed on the chalkboard board and then the instructions were given. We had a minute to make our choices when our name was called. As programs were filled, they were taken off the board, making it even more competitive for the remaining programs to choose from.

The first student was on the clock, and within seconds, they made their choice of a top surgical residency program during a prime month. Then all eyes were on me. I knew my choice, but nobody else knew what program I was choosing. I waited until the very last second to make my choice. I wanted to see those students who were not so kind to me sweat. When I said South

Dakota, the quiet room burst into laughing and finger-pointing. I heard comments like he could have had this program, and he did not take it. What a stupid decision. It did not matter what they said about me. I had the program I wanted, and now it was up to me to **Show Them** why I chose this program. I filled in my other choices, and I was set for my fourth-year externships.

Reflection

I measure my character by the promises I keep, and I will bend fear, fatigue, and circumstance before I break my word. Facing the nearness of death and the noise of other people's opinions taught me the same truth from two angles: life is precious, purpose is chosen, and courage is quiet. My father's simple faith, the aching insight that what we fear isn't pain but the separation from touch and those we love, and the promise I kept to my brother reframed survival as stewardship—of time, relationships, and integrity. Sharing my near-death experience despite skepticism, and choosing the South Dakota externship while others laughed, proved that honoring my inner compass matters more than chasing applause.

The lessons: ask your parents the questions you have while you still can; keep promises even when it costs; trust the nudge to act; and let hardship become empathy that serves others.

Approach life by staying present to what truly matters—people, purpose, and health—simplify when fear rises, choose conviction over consensus, and turn every setback into a story of service and growth.

In that posture, pain becomes wisdom, ridicule becomes fuel, and your path becomes your proof.

CHAPTER 7

The Two Greatest Words: "Thank You"

*Learning is the only thing the mind never exhausts
never fears and never regrets.*

— Leonardo Da Vinci

I made it to my fourth year of medical school. This was going to be my year, a time to shine in the clinic, no more cramming for an exam, and no more sitting in a lecture. This year, I would be traveling the country and sleeping where I could find a place to rest my head. I was excited to start this new school year.

Fourth Year Medical School, June 1996: Biomechanics Externship in San Francisco

Transition from a third-year student into a fourth-year student was a near-death experience; one day you have your physical body and within a second you don't. There was not much time to transition, as my first month was with Dr Morris, the Chief of Biomechanics soon taught me. I spent a lot of time with him over the past few years at school. His famous saying was this: "I don't care if you can do surgery, know your damn anatomy." He was referring to every time you cut on something, you'd better know the biomechanical effects that will happen after you make the correction. He pounded this concept every time he lectured.

He gave me the keys to the Residency room and told me that I was acting as the resident, and you would oversee the patients and orthotic lab. "Oh, did I tell you there are no other residents this month? You're it," he added, as the keys dropped into my hand.

Talk about baptism by fire, but I was on cloud nine. I had responsibility and the keys to the lab. I loved biomechanics. I did a lot of casting and making the orthotics in the lab. I asked a lot of questions. The one thing I was intrigued with was the ability to manipulate the foot. Dr Morris only explained this once in class and said this is the black snake whip technique. I have no idea where that name came from; I was more intrigued about how to do it. He explained to have the patient place their knee on a chair and face the opposite direction from you. You then take the foot with your thumbs on the plantar surface of the Calcaneocuboid joint. When you know they are already relaxed, you whip it in and down. Little did I know I would be using this later on in the year, and this one patient's whole career was based on this one manipulation.

July 1996: San Francisco General Hospital ER

Staying in San Francisco, I chose San Francisco General Hospital. It became one of my favorite rotations. The Head Resident at San Francisco General was my team leader. I was treated just like one of her medical residents and students. We covered the Emergency Room and the AIDS Floor, along with patients who were admitted to the hospital floor.

My first real hospital experience was working in the ER at San Francisco General. The hours were very long. I was assigned a team, and we met each morning and rounded on patients first thing, then we were given assignments. I did not know how I would be treated, as I was the only podiatry student in our group. I did not put much thought into it, and just looked at myself as I was one of them.

They allowed me to do full history and physicals. I recall one day the head resident said to me, "I would like for you to do a history and physical on this patient who is dying, and then report back to me when you're done." I approached the room with the thought of why I am doing a history and physical on a patient who is dying. She was a nice lady. I explained who I was and told her why I was there. I admit I passed on the cavity exams, but did everything else. I then reported back to the head resident. She did end up passing away while on this rotation.

Most of the students would do their medical things, and I would follow them for most of the day. There was one patient who came into the ER. He was unconscious, and I was assigned to him from start to finish. The attending and I did a lot of tests on him. When he woke up the next morning, he was having difficulty speaking. As the medical team discussed his situation, I noticed that the patient was trying to say something, so I asked the attending if I could spend some time with him; she was thrilled.

I sat by his bedside for hours, then he just started to speak. He was worried that he had AIDS. He also told me he had no family, his parents had passed away, and he was the only child. He worked on a ship for most of his life at sea. He asked me if I could go with him to get the CT scan that was ordered for him. It seemed he felt more comfortable having me there.

When the report came back, it showed he was filled with cancer. The attending told me that I was the one to tell him and that he only had about a month to live. That was hard for me to do; I felt it was up to God to take the patient when it was his time, not a doctor telling him when he was going to die. I finally informed him that he had cancer and that he did not have much time to live. He was at peace with the diagnosis, and it puzzled me: "Here is a man going to die, and yet he was relieved he did not have AIDS."

I then left for a new program. I checked back to see how he was doing a month later, and I was told he had passed away. I was sad to hear of his passing. I wonder what it was like for him, being alone and with no family by his bedside. But I also knew he was in a place of peace and did not have to worry about AIDS or anything else that troubled his mind.

August 1996, Hot Springs, VA, South Dakota: My Lottery Pick Program

I loaded up my car and made the long drive to Hot Springs, South Dakota. When I got there, I was housed on campus and worked in the hospital, the mental clinic, and the operative room. I did not get a lot of hands-on surgical experience, which was reserved for the first-year residents. I patiently observed and asked questions. But I knew I wanted this type of program as it was out in the country and had a laid-back atmosphere.

I had the chance to go and work on the Indian Reservation in Kyle. It was one of the poorest reservations in the country. Patients would walk hours to the clinic to have an ulceration on the bottom of their foot looked at, but only to be treated and then walk back home. To me, it was pointless because by the time they made it back home, either the bandages would be gone, or the ulceration would be bigger. We had to really fine-tune our clinical skills to help the people there.

I spent a lot of time with all the specialties and became good friends with the radiologist. I learned his boy was one of the top basketball players for his high school team. I expressed that I had a strong interest in basketball, so he invited me to travel to a Friday night game. I sat there and watched his boy play. I made a few recommendations on his shot, like placing the elbow closer to the body and allowing the ball to come off the middle and index fingers, and making sure the feet are pointing to the basket as the ball will follow. I was later told that not only did his field goal percentage go up, but he was also honored with being an all-conference player.

I did break away one weekend and drove back to Utah to be the best man for Corona's wedding. It was a long drive, and the night of his wedding, we were up preparing a very large pig and four little piglets that my family gifted to his family for the aloha dinner celebration for all the guests. The large hole was dug in the backyard of his fiancée's house. The pigs were laid in the pit with all the preparation. It was the best-tasting pork that I had ever eaten.

With interviews looming, choices about the future began to shape my next moves.

With the interviewing process for residency just around the corner, and due to the limited time to physically being able to visit all the programs that I was interested in, I carefully processed which programs I would visit and which ones I would interview with. I really like the Program in South Dakota and placed it as my number one program. I went and visited other programs on the East Coast and went and spent a few days traveling in Georgia and Alabama. I was interested in Tuskegee VA Hospital and the Army base in Georgia.

From the plains to the desert, the next stop promised high surgical volume and new expectations.

September 1996: Tucson VA Hospital, Arizona

This was a program that I really wanted also and took my chances on by placing it high on my list to extern with before interviews. It was a heavily sought-after program because of the surgery exposure, with the airbase being a part of the program. I live on the military base and would scrub in on cases at the base.

At the VA hospital, it was more academic. I did everything in my power to impress the attendees. This program also introduced me to how pharmaceutical companies would put on these lavish dinners to get you to use their drugs on patients. This one time, I was invited to one of these dinners, but I had to wear a tie. I don't think I had bought myself any clothes in years, so this was something very new for me. I went to the mall, bought a tie, and went to dinner. I still have that same tie.

This program allowed me to take a day off I did not tell them what for, as I did not want to harm my chances of getting into the program, but I went and took the National Boards Part I for the third time. I had scheduled it months before in a testing center. I missed passing by 2 points in a different subject that I had previous passed in my last attempt. All I could think about they would let me graduate without passing the National Boards Part I. It was so difficult being out of basic science for a year and a half and trying to remember all that stuff. I just put it in God's hands and went on to my other externships and put my focus on passing the National Boards Part II, which was coming up in the early spring.

October 1996: San Antonio, Texas, University of Health Science Center

Do you remember me talking about the Black Snake Whip technique? Well, I got to use it here.

I loved working at Lackland Air Force Base. One day, I was told to go and work this patient up. I was informed that today was his last day as an active-duty enlistee. He had this pain in his foot that no one could figure out. As I listened to him, I said, I heard of this one technique of manipulation that I was taught by one of my attendings back in school. "Have you done it before?" he asked. I confirmed, "No, but I could try." He said they have tried everything else, so he allowed me to try.

I had him get up off his chair, face towards the wall so his knee was on the chair with his foot dangling, I then took the foot, and with the memory of what I have seen over a year ago, I re-counted the technique and acted on it when I felt he was relaxed, as I executed the manipulation, I heard a big pop, and so did he. I then said, "OK, put your shoes on." He did and exclaimed, "Oh damn, there is no more pain in my foot." I went and told the attending that he had no pain; the look on his face was like he saw a deer in a headlight. I don't know what happened to him. All I knew was that the black snake whip worked! I had no idea that this simple manipulation would be the foundation for what was to come into my private practice,

One of the first surgeries I got to perform as a student in a hospital setting came on this rotation. I was given the instruments, instructed on what to do. I performed the surgery in a step-by-step manner as instructed.

Yet amid the clinical wins, an encounter would test my values and voice.

On my hospital rotation, I was assigned to this patient. We again had a team of students rounding on patients. One day, I went in early to talk with my patient, and he had told me he had soiled his medical gown that happened several days ago, and nobody had helped him. I took more information; he told me that his stomach was not feeling good.

When the team showed up to see the patient, the attending asked how number such and such. I said, "You mean Mr. Smith." The attending did not like that I called the patient by his name. He was not just a patient with a number to me; he was a human being just like the rest of us. Today, he was Mr. Smith and was a patient seeking medical help. I told the team that he needed an internal medicine consultation due to his diarrhea. And the elective surgery should be postponed that was scheduled for the following day. As the medical team went off to the next patient, I stayed behind to help the patient with his soiled gown. The attending turned back and asked, "Glen, are you coming with us?" I said, "This patient needs help with his soiled gown." He said, "Doctors do not change bed sheets; that is for the nurses, so come with us now." I looked at the patient and said I am sorry, and with my head pointed to the floor in frustration and sorrow followed me out of the room with the medical team.

The next day, I showed up to do clinical rounds. I was given a note from the front desk that I was relieved of my duty on the floor. "Relieved of my duties? Where is my patient?" I asked. They said I have no assigned patients, and the attending said I can take the rest of the week off. I again asked where my patient was. The staff informed me they took him into surgery, but the last time I heard, he is now in the intensive care unit, fighting for his life. I don't know what happened to the patient, but I had to leave the floor as instructed. I went to another part of the clinic and worked.

As the month closed, a candid hallway conversation reshaped how I evaluated programs.

On my last day at this rotation in San Antonio, I was walking down a long hallway with the head attending, and he asked me, "What do you think about our program here? Would you like to be a resident here?" I was about to answer him, but his phone rang; he started talking on the phone as we walked. I patiently waited for him to get off his phone before he asked me what I thought about his program. As I went to answer him, his phone rang again. Once again, I patiently waited until he got off his phone. He asked a third time what I thought about the program, but this time I waited for his phone to ring. He said, "Are you not going to answer my question?" I said, "I am just waiting for your phone to ring again. I see you are a very busy man."

He turned his phone off as we continued walking, then asked, "So, what do you think about our program? Would you like to be a resident here?" I flatly said no.

I probably was the first student to ever say no to him. He asked why; without going into details of my previous experience with one of his head residents, I just responded by saying there is no biomechanics here. He asked, "So you like biomechanics? Well, come with me then."

We went into the sports medicine clinic; he told the head resident to step aside and let Dr Robison work this patient up, and then have him cast the patient for orthotics. While they observed me, I worked the patient up and made the cast molds for the orthotics, and then laid the cast on the table. The attending and his resident came over and picked up the molds and looked at them, and motioned me to step outside. He was impressed.

"If you come to our program, I will make sure we have a biomechanics lab, and you will oversee it. Would you be interested?"

I declined and thanked him again. I could not see myself in a program that looked at patients as numbers. I did not want to come back to a program and work with the previous head resident, who would still be at the program.

It was the only clinical program that I did not get an A in; they gave me a B because I was not considered a team player. Interesting, because all my patients came first, and I only spoke up when I felt they were in harm's way. I still felt that the patient who had diarrhea needed to be seen by Internal medicine before surgery, and if that meant I got a lower grade for speaking up, I would gladly accept the B for my grade.

The grade I received reflected their view of teamwork, but I measured success by advocacy.

First Interview for Residency Program: How Do You Castrate Pigs?

I went to my first interviews for residency programs. In preparation for getting programs to catch my interest for an interview, I had to come up with a plan to set myself apart from everyone else, since my grades were subpar, and I was at the bottom of the class for class rankings. I could not use my academics as my strong point. The one thing that was my strong point was my experience. You were required to write a 200-word summary as to why the residency program would give you an interview.

This is what I wrote:

"If you are going to be a surgeon, you'd better learn how to cut skin, as my dad handed me his pocketknife with blood dripping off the blade. He said. "Go to it." I had never castrated a piglet, but looking over all the little pigs that needed to be fixed, I did what I had observed. I made the cut in the skin, squeezed out the testicle and teased it down, and then cut it off, while the piglet was screaming and squealing, then I would proceed to find the other testicle and do the same procedure. I concluded that your program will give me my dream of becoming a surgeon. Just as I first experienced on the farm."

I got interested in residency programs for interviews, and even one told me they were only interested in how I castrated piglets.

November 1996: San Diego, CA MCRD (Marine Corps Recruit Depot)

One of my first real hands-on experiences in a major clinical setting was at the naval base in San Diego, where I would help with the recruits as they came in. Boy, was I thankful I was a civilian. I got to experience more surgery at Balboa Naval Hospital. I still remember the room and the foot we were working on as if it were just yesterday.

I had to respond as to whether to go to the interviews in Los Angeles. I did not have the money even to pay for the ride up to Los Angeles. The house where I was staying had a saying of the day on the kitchen table. It said, "Don't spend money for no worth."

I had to trust my decision not to interview at the Los Angeles interviews. I still felt South Dakota would come through. I listed South Dakota as my #1 spot, Tucson as my number #2 spot, and then Denver as my #3, and Alabama as my #4. I made a call to the residency director in South Dakota, but had to leave a message for him. I told him I am listing your program number 1. I later found out that the message was never delivered to him. I also learned that there were over 900 applicants who ranked this program, and there were only four spots available. It was now it was a waiting game.

December 1996: Denver, Colorado VA Hospital

I spent a month at the VA hospital in Denver. What I remember is spending time with the patient after hours. I did this for the main reason to improve my skills in communicating with patients.

Secondly, I rented a bedroom from a fellow resident, who happened to be female. Had my parents known that I was sharing an apartment with a female, all crap would have hit the fan for religious reasons. I did not see her much with her schedule, and I was out working in the clinic most of the time; I just needed a bed to rest my head on.

This program taught me a lot about listening to patients. Ever since my experience in San Antonio, I wanted to be a better doctor and truly listen to the patients. I felt the longer I listened, the quicker I could find the diagnosis.

January 1997: Sacaton Indian Reservation, Arizona

The Indian reservation with Dr Yamada was a great turning point in my education. Day one, I was assigned patients in the hospital, and we would treat them from head to toe, order the labs, and report to the attending. I remember they were moving from the old clinic to a brand-new clinic. It was a weekend, which happened to be my birthday. I spent all day Saturday and Sunday moving everything over to the new clinic. The doctor did not know that it was my birthday, but later found out somehow.

When he showed up on Monday, everything was ready to go; there were no delays in seeing patients. I think working at the local grocery store and organizing all the shelves and produce, and coolers gave me an upper hand on setting up this clinic. The doctor at the end of the rotation expressed to me that he wanted me as his resident, and even with him filling all the slots, he was going to make room for me if I wanted the program. But because the ranking system was finalized, and I was ranked low on his list, we did not match. When I learned I was headed to South Dakota, all the preparation paid off. I had been ranked in the top 4 of the 900-plus applicants, and I was so excited to go there.

While on the reservation externship, I had a good roommate who got into one of the military residency programs. I must have vented my frustration out loud with my schooling and not knowing if I would even be allowed to graduate. He got me out of my head by taking me to the movies up in the city and watching movies like *The Adventures of Beavis and Butthead*. He got me to laugh, which I needed; the movie alone was dumb enough to put a smile on my face. One night, he took me outside and asked me to look up. I looked up at the vast sky. He said, "What do you see?" I said that it is a buttload of stars.

"Now that is where you go wrong. Try focusing on just one star in the sky, and you won't feel so overwhelmed in life."

February 1997: San Francisco, CA General Community Medicine

The one experience that stands out the most here was while on a Neurological rotation at a Seton Medical hospital in the Bay Area, the Attending asked me to come with him as we had a new patient. He was hang gliding, and he hit a cliff, so we had to go and assess him to see if he was alive. We entered a room where the patient was lying in bed; he was hooked up to a machine and seemed to be very normal. In my mind, I could only imagine blood everywhere; half of a face, a limb missing, but this patient just lay in bed with a tube in his mouth. The doctor said this is how we assess if someone is dead, and he went step by step. The last one was turning off the machine that supplied the oxygen to him to see the brain activity, and it was flat. He said this patient is dead.

Now I need to tell the family. I walked with the doctor to the reception area, where he met the family. I stayed behind the not-so-private wall and listened to the doctor explain that their child was dead. He then went on to explain that if they would consent to have his vital organ donated, as there was a waiting list of patients wanting kidneys, lungs, heart, and everything else from an organ donor. After the papers were signed, we proceeded to finish our rounds. The next lady we came to was on a machine. The doctor said, "Here is the opposite of what you just experienced. She has been brain-dead for years, but the family wishes to keep her alive, and so we must honor that. Then he turns off the machine and says, "See, she is dead, there is no brain activity." Then he turned the machine back on and said, "We will honor the family request."

This brought me back to a memory of a lady that I met in Washington when I was on my mission for my church. She was on a machine for 21 years after being struck by lightning. She came back to life with her full memory intact, and she was puzzled as to why her church no longer lectured in Latin. Still, she was now giving service in English, and she was also a grandma to her daughter's child. So, I have mixed feelings seeing these two cases. I had just seen a young man in his prime who had just died a few hours ago from head trauma, and then I saw a lady who was being kept alive with the hope and wishes of the family.

Next month, National Boards Part II will be just around the corner. I had to put the National Boards Part I to the back of my mind and focus on and study the clinical aspects of the National Boards.

March 1997: Oakland, CA, Highland General Hospital

Oakland: Upon returning to the nearby city where the medical school was located, I took a rotation with a county hospital in Oakland. I remember one day a gentleman came in with chronic ingrown toenails; the head doctor requested that a head resident take over the case. I responded that it was not necessary and that I could handle it. She was impressed with my confidence, so she allowed me to numb up the toe, take out a surgical blade, make two half-moon incisions, and remove the entire nail matrix, and then suture the skin back together, and bandaging, with no one helping me.

Another patient came in with a fracture. I once again declined the head resident's help and applied a fiberglass cast to the patient's leg. The attending doctor told me that I was unrecognizable from when I was a student, whom she had in her class, to now, the student who is doing resident work as a 4th-year student. She was impressed. Confidence from the clinic carried me into the testing center.

National Boards Part II: Is This My Time to Shine?

I went into the testing center to take my National Boards Part II. I felt more confident as the questions were more clinical and not basic science. The test was set up the same way you take the set of questions, and if the test felt you needed more, it would tell you to go on to the next set of questions until you came to the 5th set of questions. I prepared differently; I relaxed before the test, and I even went sailing on the San Francisco Bay with some friends the day before the test, which was far from relaxing, as it scared the hell out of me. Still, I did experience it, and I can say I have gone sailing once in my life. Maybe sailing took every ounce of fear out of my body, so I did not fear the test.

While I was in the testing center, I finished the first part of the test, and it told me to move on to the next one. All the thoughts of the National Boards Part I started to come into my mind. I took a breath and let all those fears and anxieties leave my body before I proceeded, even though I was being timed. I started to answer the questions, and then it said, "You're done right after the first set of questions. You can exit the test and see your score."

My heart was really racing now. I know I could not go back and redo the test with some of the questions that I guessed on, so I hit the button, and it said: "Congratulations, you scored an accumulative score of 92 percent." I passed the National Boards Part II.

April 1997: Las Vegas, Nevada Mentorship at a Private Practice

I spent a month with a private practice doctor in Las Vegas. I spent a lot of time in the clinic and in surgery with him; he was very respected, and his patients loved him. It was my first time having to develop X-rays from film in a black room, dipping the film in one solution and then to the next until finished.

He had a secretary who was very good at what she did. She told me her husband goes golfing, and so I met up with him and went golfing. When I visited their home, they were loading up their newly born Shih Tzu puppies to take them to the vet. They were a breed that was born with one extra toe on each paw, and these toes (digits) needed to come off. One of the family members said to me, "Hey, you're a foot doctor, you can remove the toes."

I did not realize she was serious, but she took the four puppies and laid them on the kitchen table. I said to myself, if I can castrate piglets, then I can obviously remove a small toe on a puppy. I took out my medical bag and performed amputation of each of the extra digits on each paw and bandaged them. A few weeks later, the veterinarian called to ask why they did not show up. They said, "Oh, we took them to a podiatrist."

I kept in touch with that family for some time. The mother took ill several years after I was in private practice and passed away. I drove up to her funeral. Leaving the funeral and on the way home, the radio would come in and out of songs being played. I started to put the words together, and it was as if she was saying some-thing to me. I had driven that road many times, and still to this day, which is the only time that this has happened. I will greatly miss her. I loved her contagious smile and her pleasant demeanor, and I miss the spontaneous golfing trip with her husband.

May 1997: Logan, Utah, Delivering Flowers for Rudy's Greenhouse

Every student was given a month off to visit programs. I put so much trust and faith into the South Dakota program, I planned to take my month off the very last month of my schooling, when I should have taken it off in the prime months, to visit programs. So, while everyone was doing their externships at various programs, that really did not mean much. I was delivering flowers for Rudy Greenhouse in Logan, Utah. I went and lived on the floor of my brother's apartment at Utah State for about three weeks. They helped me find a job delivering flowers to local grocery store chains. I loved staying busy while everyone was at school. I was given the job of delivering flowers across Northern Utah and Idaho, and even into Wyoming.

They would load the truck up the night before, and I would go in at about 4 a.m. and drive the delivery to the various cities. I would want to be at the stores before they opened their doors. There were several times I would do multiple deliveries in one day. I know some of the workers who had been there for years were a little jealous of me, as it was the sought-after job to deliver the flowers. I was not much affected by this, and every time I would work in the greenhouse, the owner would find me and ask me to take the delivery.

One day, I clocked a 21-hour day of straight driving and delivery. After three weeks, the owner, to show his appreciation, handed me a 100-dollar bill out of his pocket and said thank you. I finished up at the greenhouse and went back home to help my father for a few days before graduation.

Letter of Appreciation to My High School Counselor

I finished school with a 2.78 GPA. Just under a B average, but I never failed a class. I only ended up with 3 D's but like Jared said, D stands for Doctor, and I was ok with it. I had accomplished the unthinkable, and I was ready to receive my Doctorate Degree in Podiatric Medicine. Even though I had not passed my National Boards Part I, I still was able to graduate with my class.

Do you remember the high school counselor who told me that I would never make it into college? I sent him a graduation announcement and thanked him for telling me I could not do it. I thanked him for saying, "Good luck getting into college." I said to him, "I will be walking with my cap and gown and will be receiving a medical degree in Podiatry, and I plan on becoming a surgeon." I added, "Be careful to whom you tell, they can't do it, because most will believe you, as you are their guidance counselor. As for me, I happened to be one of the lucky ones who did not listen to your recommendation, and for that, I am truly grateful to you."

I created the drive and determination to go to college, and look where I made it. I **SHOWED HIM** I could do it. With that chapter closed, the moment I had chased for years finally arrived.

Graduation Ceremony: All Students Were All Equal on Stage

I had asked my father if he would go to my graduation from medical school, and his response was always, "Yes, I will go if I am still around. Still, I will probably be dead by then." He always told me he was going to die before my graduation. I had a few days before graduation. I spent it at the cemetery taking care of the grounds that our family oversaw. I mowed everything, so there was no excuse for him not to go. I asked my uncle for the use of his van and told my dad we needed to go to California. I did all the driving. My brother Clark and his wife joined us on the trip, along with my other brother Mark. We stayed at a family home in San Jose, CA, and we drove up to the graduation ceremony. My stomach was in knots, with excitement and anticipation. I placed the doctorate gown and cap on and eagerly waited for my name to be called. I walked across the stage, signifying that I had just done the unthinkable: "I was officially a doctor." My father and mother had the biggest smiles that I had ever seen before. They were indeed proud parents.

The emotions in my mind were so overwhelming that even a tear sprang free from the corner of my eye and slowly proceeded down my face. I said my goodbyes to my classmates who helped me. I am truly grateful for all the experiences that I had to go through. When my knees found the floor that evening, I just thanked him for everything and did not ask anything in return. It was a prayer of gratitude.

Glen and Corona medical school graduation San Francisco CA.

Glen with mom and dad medical school Graduation San Francisco CA.

Reflection

Looking back on my fourth year, I see a path paved by grit, humility, and faith–learning to show up early, stay late, listen longer, and do the right thing even when it costs me. From biomechanics labs to ER goodbyes, from reservations to recruit depots, from failing and trying again to finally passing, I learned that skill matters, but character matters more: know your anatomy, advocate for your patients, honor people by their names, and never be too proud to change a patient's soiled gown. I learned to focus on one star when life feels overwhelming, to trust preparation when outcomes are uncertain, and to let setbacks refine–not define–me. The black snake whip taught me that small, precise actions can change a life; long drives and longer nights taught me that gratitude grows in hard places; mentors and doubters taught me to believe, work, and keep moving.

I will approach life with the same resolve: serve first, listen deeply, choose integrity over approval, embrace discomfort as the price of growth, and give thanks–because every step, even the painful ones, can become part of a purpose bigger than myself.

CHAPTER 8

A Surgeon's Life Begins

At the center of your being, you have the answer.
You know who you are, and you know what you want.

— Lao Tzu

5th Time's a Charm: Taking My National Boards Part I for the Last Time

Prior to heading off to my residency program, my best friend, Corona, wanted to surprise me with a gift. He wanted to take me to Hawaii to see where he was raised after moving from Tonga. I enjoyed seeing the place where he was raised and where he went to school. He also showed me some of the local places that he would go to. The food was so good, I don't know what it was, but my tongue agreed to it. Once I got back from Hawaii, there was not much time before I loaded up my car and made the drive to South Dakota. The main residency was moved to Sturgis and was no longer in Hot Springs. I settled into an apartment in Rapid City and could not wait to meet the director and the other residents. Our residency program was divided into various programs (Podiatry, General Surgery, Orthopedics, Internal Medicine, Radiology, and many more).

I volunteered to do the Podiatry rotations first, while the other residents were doing their non-Podiatry rotations. I chose Podiatry first because I still needed to pass the National Boards Part I, and I could take a day off to travel to take the test, because there was another resident helping in the podiatry clinic.

I located the nearest testing center in South Dakota that was in Sioux Falls, a good five-hour drive from Rapid City. On Friday, July

11[th,] I drove to Sioux Falls after the clinic. Exhausted from the previous day of clinic and the long drive, I arrived in Sioux Falls after midnight and found a cheap hotel to fall asleep, but to be honest with you, I did not sleep much; my mind was too busy worrying about the test. I arrived at the testing center a little early, like I always do. I checked in, found my place in front of the computer, and started the test.

I finished the first set of questions, but it helped me continue to the next set of questions. Thinking in my mind, here we go again, just like all the past three exams. It had me go through the entire set of questions, as all the previous tests did. When I finished the set of questions, I clicked the box that says, "see my score." It then showed a message: "Sorry, you did not pass. You got a 74 percent in one subject; here is your breakdown."

Just like clockwork, I had failed the subject that I passed before and passed the subject I failed the previous test. One subject just kept keeping me from passing that damn test! The ultimate frustration set in. I had passed every single subject, but because of the way the test was set up, I once again failed by only one subject. I had worked my ass off; I did everything that was left in my tank. I was ready to go back to Rapid City, pack my bags, and leave a note to my fellow resident asking him to please give this to the Director of the residency program. Thank goodness the drive back to Rapid City was long because it allowed me to talk myself back into the program and stick with it. I said to myself, there must be another option to take this test. When I got back, I quickly jumped onto the computer and found that the test was offered one more time, but in Casper, Wyoming, on September 11th.

Having the test fresh in my mind, I just started to write out every single question that I could think of in every subject. If I did not fully know the question, I would study it. There was no need to study material that I already knew, so I focused the next two months fine-tuning the questions that caused me to think and guess at an answer. I did not have the time to study everything from the past, starting 4 years ago when my basic science classes started.

Because the test was on a Thursday, I had to ask to take a few days off. I did not want to drive late at night after the clinic as I did before, so I asked for Wednesday off and Thursday. I did not study at all the day before the test, and I had a good dinner before I fell asleep on a hotel bed. I went to bed early and woke up refreshed, but the anxiety was still there; who wouldn't if this one test determined my entire career? I was over $232,000 in student loan debt, and to find a new career that would pay for this monthly expense only made me more anxious and frustrated. If I knew you could declare bankruptcy on student loans, more than likely, I would have given up sooner. There was only one option, and that was to pass that damn test. I had to put my trust in God that it would all work out.

I arrived at the testing center, I was directed to the computer, and I was the only one in the room, so I could literally yell if I wanted to. I was given a blank piece of paper and a pencil and started the test. After finishing the main block of questions, it told me to proceed. Every foul word came to mind, even the words for which my brother beat me up. I calmed my mind and said to myself, "You got this, just proceed, Glen."

After I finished the next section, it had me proceed to the next. I knew I had three more sections after this one, so I answered every question that they asked me. When I finished the last section and was told to stop and exit the test to see my score, I was speechless because either I really bombed it, or I passed. I just stared at that screen like a deer in a headlight. Do I want to know my fate or not? I placed the arrow over the exit button and closed my eyes, and clicked the button. There was complete silence as I opened just one eye to peek at the screen.

I saw the words "**CONGRATULATIONS,** you passed." I reviewed all the subjects, and I got an accumulative score of over 90 percent. The impossible has just been defeated. Nothing now was going to stop me from becoming a foot and ankle surgeon.

I now felt I was officially graduated, and I felt I was like every-one on that stage who got their diploma. I was a Doctor of Podiatric Medicine, and nobody could take that away from me. I had earned it! As painful as this was for me, it was a life lesson in perseverance. I don't think there ever was a medi-cal student before or, in that manner, a medical student in the future who took this test five times over a period of two years. Perseverance was there to show me that impossible things in life are possible, as long as you stay persistent. I was so excited to drive back to Rapid City and work in the clinic. The only thing I had to do before heading back was to tell God thanks for getting me through this.

Please Remove This Cast from My Leg; My Wife Can't Sleep

I finished up my Podiatry rotations and was eagerly ready to start my orthopedic rotations at the airbase. The two main programs I was looking forward to were the orthopedics at Ellsworth Air Force Base and the general surgery rotation at the VA hospital.

One day at the airbase, an adult patient came in with a broken leg. The attending told me to put on a cast. I asked the patient what color he would like for his cast, and he said, "Surprise me." So, I proceeded to put on a glow-in-the-dark white casting material as my first layer, then I took a smaller 2-inch red casting material and made his leg like a candy cane. It was perfect for the holi-day season that we were in. He thought it looked cool, then when he came back sooner than his scheduled time to have the cast removed. He said, "You've got to take this cast off, my wife is yell-ing at me every night, she says she can't sleep because the cast you put on glows in the dark."

I think the one thing that fascinated me the most with this rota-tion was the arm and hand surgery that I got to sit in on. I did not get credit for these, as I could only record foot and ankle cases for my residency. Still, I never turned down an opportunity to see something that I would never see again. I noticed the hand was a lot like the foot. The tendons, bones, and arteries all look the same once you uncover the skin.

One of the orthopedic doctors that I worked with told me this: "If you want to be successful in practice, use the three A's of success: Availability, Affability, and your Ability in that order." This has proven to work. Patients want to be seen as soon as possible, and they want to be heard, and lastly is they look at your ability, or nowadays, Google reviews, which did not exist when I was a resident.

It Pays to Pray: How God Moved My Vehicle from Incoming Traffic

Nervous as all get out with starting my general surgery rotation, and a little shaken by what had just taken place on my way to the morning rounds. When I hit a patch of black ice on the freeway shooting my vehicle across the frost-bitten grass in the median and right towards oncoming traffic. By the act of God, my truck turned quickly, missing the oncoming traffic at the same time, keeping all four tires on the road. How I did not roll that vehicle, or let alone miss the traffic, was only because of my prayer that morning when I prayed for safety before leaving my apartment.

As I walked into the introductions of general surgery, whose main attending was a rough old military doctor who frequently took smoke breaks between surgeries, the first word that came out of the attending surgeon's mouth was "I don't know why in the hell they keep sending your type here to my floor. You need to go back to Podiatry." I responded, "Treat me like I am no different than your general surgeon students. But if I may just for today be excused for the day, I was in a car accident just an hour ago."

After being excused for the day, I showed up bright and early the next day. It was as if I were in the army. It did not help matters that the general surgeon who happened to be my attending was an old Vietnam vet who put people back together. I was given my orders for the day. After working up full physicals on patients who were going into surgery, and making sure everything was ready for tomorrow's surgery, I spent many hours just going over the material to make sure everything was ready. When my regular day was done, I was off to the emergency room, which they did not require, but because I had worked in the ER in San Francisco, I wanted to see what a country ER was like. The attending did not turn my desires down and welcomed an extra pair of hands to help.

One of the first patients was a man who came in with his finger severely cut from a band saw. That same night, a lady came into the ER with her skull exposed. The lady had been kicked in the face with her horse and had split the skin right down to the skull from her nose to her forehead. The doctor threw one stitch and then said, "Finish the rest." I carefully pinched the two sides of the skin together and made my way up the face, closing in the exposed skull that was staring me in the face. It was my goal to make her face so there would be no scars. I don't know how she ended up, and that was the last time I saw her. Working in the emergency room kept me on my toes and always learning and studying for responses to quick-thinking experiences. I was so thankful for the time I had at San Francisco General Hospital and working in the emergency room.

Get Me That Damn LDS Retractor (and I Don't Mean Learning Disability Student!)

Over the course of several months, I started to win the trust of the general surgeon. I would scrub in on major cases, such as bowel obstructions, open heart procedures, abdominal aortas, removing kidneys, and hernia repairs. I was fascinated when I saw my first live heart pumping in the chest cavity that was recently cracked open.

On one occasion, we were in a major case where the bowel obstruction was extreme, the surgeon called for an LDS retractor, and the scrub nurse was frazzled with each request. I could see the general surgeon getting more and more impatient. After he said, "Get me that damn LDS retractor." I said through my surgical mask, "I am right here." I could only see his eyes, looking at me from across the table, then there was a small chuckle under his mask. The scrub nurse found the retractor, and we went on to finish the surgery.

Pillsbury Blue Boy

We had an early morning case. It was cold getting to work, and now they were blasting the cooler in the operative room. I was trying to find ways to stay warm. Often, they would take the blankets that was in a heater and place on the patients, and even sometimes on themselves to stay warm in the operative room. Still on pins and needles with the attending and trying to find ways to stay warm while waiting for him, I asked one of the operative staff if she could hand me the hose that was used to inflate a warm shield around the patient. She asked what I needed it for. I said, "Watch"; I tucked in the pant legs in my socks and closed off my shirt sleeves, then I stuck the hose into my upper chest scrubs and told the staff to turn on the machine. I was literally a walking Pillsbury blue boy; I was finally warm. Then the attending walked into the room. In his military voice, he said, "Enough of the horseplay, the patient is ready for surgery." So I went out and scrubbed for the case.

On one occasion, I was notified by the general surgeon to follow him. We went through many passageways to the basement of the hospital. I did not know that it even existed. But as we pulled the fresh body out of the cooler, the doctor said this patient died yesterday. We have to find out why. "Have you ever done an autopsy?" I said, "No, but I have spent many years working on cadavers."

He said, "Well, the only difference is there is no embalming fluid yet, so you will do just fine." We sawed open his skull to see the brain, cracked open his chest to see the lungs, and then we opened up his abdomen to see the intestines. Another "damn it!" from the doctor. "Do you see that?" Pointing to the area, he explained, "Well, that is what killed him. I must now go and write up the report and tell the family. Could you please close everything for me?" I said, "No problem." So I spent the next few hours putting the chest back together, placing the brain back in the skull, and closing the skin with each stick as if I was in surgery and placed him back in the cooler.

From that point on, I was asked to be his first assistant. On my last day of the rotation, the doctor called me into his office. He said, "I have enjoyed having you in my surgery. In fact, you are one of two students that I really enjoyed teaching in my career. If you want to go and become a general surgeon, I can help you. I sit on the admission board at the medicine school that supplies us, the students. Just let me know if you are interested."

The thought of going back to school, but sitting in the general science courses, and taking the boards was not favorable, plus I wanted to marry and have children one day, and I did not want to be married to my work; this was the main reason why I chose to decline his offer. I thanked him and said I loved what I do as a podiatrist. He said, "Well, if you reconsider, let me know." We spent the remaining time looking at old war slides and hearing the stories of people getting blown up by landmines.

It was not the last time I scrubbed in with him and spent what time I was available to scrub in on those big cases that he needed an assistant for. He would even page me out of Internal medicine to help with some of the cases throughout my residency.

Urology: Why I Am so Thankful I am a Podiatrist

I was asked to assist other specialties, one of which was Urology. One of the cases that I almost lost it was assisting with an elderly man's circumcision. Thank goodness he was given general anesthesia. On another occasion, I assisted in removing a kidney from another patient. That was a fascinating case.

Japanese Doctor Who Wanted to See the Sand Hill Cranes Before He Retires

I had the opportunity to work with this Japanese doctor; he was very knowledgeable, spoke very few words, but boy, did he teach me with his hands and eyes. He would tap on my hand, and with a stern look, he would show me with his own hands how he wanted it done, and then he had me do it. I spent many hours in the Operative room with him.

On one occasion, while working in the skin clinic, he would talk about the sandhill cranes, and said his dream was to one day go and see them. I told him that if he could get me out of the clinic, I would drive him down to Nebraska so he could see them. He said, "OK, let's go."

So we left on a Thursday night, right after clinic, drove 8 hours, and spent a short evening in a hotel. We got up around 3 a.m. and waited for the sandhill cranes to fly in and land on the Platte River. The morning was cool. The steam was rising off the river, and then the early morning sun rose, showing its rays. The sky was magical, thousands and thousands of birds flying in and landing on the banks of the river; it was a sight that only the eyes could speak.

Hey Doc! What Kind of a Doctor Are You?

Internal medicine stretched my medical knowledge even further. After doing the San Francisco rotation at San Francisco General Hospital, I felt I was a little better prepared. I was asked to perform a history and physical on the new patients.

I remember one patient who came in; he was new to the hospital. I sat down with him; I was no longer in scrubs but in a white shirt and tie and white doctor coat, and I began to ask the basic questions. When we got to the physical, I said I needed to check your prostate. He asked, "Is that necessary?" I said yes, only because I was told to do it, and the nice thing about podiatry is you don't have to check the cavities of the body. I was instructed by my attending to do everything, so I could not skip it.

Little did the patient know that this was my first time, but I never let him know that. I was given general instructions on how to prepare for the exam and what to feel for. I was told to use my finger like a windshield wiper. When you're on the prostate, you will feel two lobes. You want to feel for the symmetrical and size, as I lubricated my finger and had the patient bend over the table with his face facing down, and then spreading the legs, I proceeded to perform the prostate examination.

While my finger was locating his prostate, he asked me, "Hey, what kind of doctor are you?" with a scratch in his voice as the finger proceeded further. I admitted that I am a podiatrist. He then asked, "A doctor who treats feet?" I said yes. He questioned, "What in the hell are you doing down there?" I said, "Your prostate is fine, and I will give the report to the attending. Your physical is finished."

I must have done well with my examinations of these new patients. The attending, who oversaw the entire internal medicine department, asked me if I would be interested in going to a camp for boys and girls. He said I would be the doctor in charge of whatever I see in the clinic. Never turning down an opportunity to learn, I said yes, and so the driver and I went to the camp clinic. It took a little over an hour to get there. It was a camp for troubled boys and girls. There was a nurse on staff, so I did have help. I saw everything from common colds to STDs (sexually transmitted diseases).

If I was not in a general surgery case or in internal medicine, I was in the Pathology lab, drawing blood from the patient and then running the chemistry panels. The staff seemed to like that I was there; they just kept giving me more and more things to do.

Anaphylaxis Attack: The Day I Helped Save a Patient's Life

I spent a short period of time at the VA hospital in Hot Springs. There, I worked with the radiologist, the same one whose son was on the basketball team that I helped with his basketball game.

The doctor said, "Would you like to go to the MRI facility and watch what I do to take an MRI?" I, of course, said yes. There was an older veteran who needed an MRI. I watched the doctor inject the contrast dye into his arm. I said I had this done to me in school. I asked if he had ever seen an allergic reaction to the dye. He spoke. "No, never, it is a rarity."

We then took the patient into the room, laid him on the table, and went into the other room and started the process. There was a window through which we could see the patient. I noticed he started to move his hand, so I told the doctor that he is reacting, but he said the movement is still normal. I repeated my observation. Luckily, he listened to me and stopped taking the views on the MRI. When he entered the room, the patient was having a full-on anaphylactic attack, just like I did. He rushed the patient into the department and called code blue. The medical team arrived and worked on him. They were able to revive him.

After all the excitement, he asked me, "How did you know? I have never seen one in my career." I explained that this is what happened to me when I was in school a few years ago. He said, "I am so thankful you were with me today. Had you not been here, he would not be hugging his wife today; we would have been consoling her and explaining that her husband had died. You saved that man's life."

I feel that going through what I had gone through paved the way for me to be there that day. Was this the reason why I needed to come to South Dakota for my residency program? I feel it was one of the reasons, among many others.

Branding Cows: A Required Course for My Residency Program

I did find time to enjoy the black hills of South Dakota. I had bought a mountain bike and would go out at times when there was no work for me to do at the hospital. I was approached by one of the staff personal and asked if I would like to go and help brand cows on a Saturday morning. I eagerly accepted the offer. "Can you meet me at this place early next Saturday morning?" he asked. "Of course," I replied. When I showed up and jumped into his truck and headed to the ranch, he began to explain that we need those cows over there and those fences over here. He explained to me the process of how he branded the cows. He asked if I had some questions. I said, "Nope, let's do it." When he saw me working the cattle and helping with the branding, he looked at me with amazement. I just smiled and said, "My father ran cattle." He said, "Oh, now I see why you were so good at this."

There was no better residency program in the country that helped shape my medical mind and ways of thinking while working with patients. I got to help with general surgery, see a live heartbeat, worked at the ER, and was entrusted with patients in Internal Medicine. What first-year Podiatry Resident could say that? I also feel it was the only program that would allow me to take time off my work schedule and go and take a test that was required to pass before going into practice, let alone a residency program. I felt truly guided and blessed. I am so thankful I chose this program over any program in the county, and all those laughs and finger-pointing, well, those were meaningless to me. If those fellow students could have seen what I did in my first year of residency, they would have taken that one slot to South Dakota.

After finishing up my first-year residency program, I didn't feel like I could go into private practice as of yet, but I was even offered a job working with an Orthopedic doctor. I felt I needed more training in Podiatric surgery, and so I applied to a surgical program out in Arizona. It did not pay, but it did give free housing. I was accepted and made plans to move out when I completed my residency program.

Second Year Surgical Residency: Valley of the Sun

In my first-year residency program, I knew I needed another year of residency; I had spent more time in general medicine than I did with surgery in Podiatry back in South Dakota. The California College of Podiatry Medicine had a nonpaying one-year surgical program. Dr. Reese was the residency director, and he had a few other attendings. This was a time when there was a shortage of residency in the country, so I was very thankful to have been selected to be one of the three residents in this program.

The program had a condominium-type place that was used for residents. It was nice not having to pay for rent, but we exchanged rent for working not only in surgery but also taking calls 24/7 and helping in clinics with various doctors' offices throughout the valley of Phoenix. The office manager was very nice and would get us things from Costco to put in our refrigerator to help with the eating costs. I knew Costco was cheap to eat as I had experienced this in med school. It is amazing how you can survive on very little.

More Seeing Than Doing: Frustrations Rising

I was becoming more frustrated with this program; I feel I could be doing more than just observing. I even thought this was the last week of my stay here; I was ready to leave the program. I guess I was so used to having the trust of the doctors in South Dakota. This surgical program, like when I was a 3rd year student, was all about watching with no hands-on training. I talked to the doctors and expressed that I would like to do more hands-on training. The doctors listened to me and started to let me do more. It is amazing what happens when you speak up.

Either Take It out or Finish Injecting

Training never stopped even if I was the one being worked on: I explained to one of the attending that my heel was hurting, he said get up on the chair, and take your shoe, he then pulled out a syringe and stuck the needle into my heel and let it dangle in my foot, and said as he walked out of the room, you can either finish it or pull it out. I did not pull the needle out, but after working out the nausea and sour stomach feeling, I proceeded to inject my heel and finished what he started. My heel has not bothered me since.

While in surgery with another attending, I was doing what I always would do in surgery: learning, observing, and hoping to do more than that. This surgeon was one who would not allow residents to do the surgery cases under supervision. He was very protective, and I don't blame him for that. In this case, when I scrubbed in, I was trying to be one step ahead of his every move to have things ready for him. As I reached across the surgical field to help with his next step, he took the surgical instrument in his hand and hit my hand so hard that it almost brought tears to my eyes. I did not say anything but stepped back, took my gloves off, and stepped out of the surgical room. I refused to go back and assist him from that point on. He asked for me, but I did not go back. I had the other resident assist him in surgery. I went and worked with other surgeons.

Because he was one of the directors of the program, he asked to talk with me. He asked, "Why did you leave that day in surgery?" I told him I did not like getting hit. "You really hurt my hand. It is just instinctively in me to be one step ahead of the surgeon in surgery to make sure everything is running smoothly. All I was doing was assisting you," I explained. He asked me if I would scrub in again. I said thank you, but no thanks. He insisted, "I would like for you to scrub in with me. Would you do that? It will be just you."

I, not wanting to fail the program, went to his surgery case. The patient was on the table and sedated. He then instructed me to do the procedure: "You're going to do it from start to finish." He handed me the surgical blade, and then his voice guided me through each step from start to finish. I thanked him for taking the time to teach me and trusting me. He said he was sorry for that day. I worked more with him until the program ended.

Release the Clamps! Is There Blood Flowing?

One of the programs I had the opportunity to experience was a vascular rotation at the VA hospital. It was a required program to complete the residency program. The head resident was very knowledgeable and fun to hang around with. He asked me one day if I wanted to assist with an Abdominal Aortic Aneurysm. I jumped at the opportunity and scrubbed in. I watched with intense eyes the process of opening up the abdominal cavity, moving and retracting all the intestines, and then identifying the aneurysm, and then switching the patient over to a machine to keep him alive.

In contrast, the aneurysm was carefully dissected, and the new graft was placed in its place. I was told to go and stand down at the end of the table. I went and stood at the end of the table. Then the clamps of the upper portion of the abdominal aorta were released, and the pressure of the blood went shooting out and covered me in blood. I stood there with blood dripping down, and I did not see the humor in it. They quickly clamped the aorta and then put the graft in and sutured it in place. They released the clamp. There were no leaks; I was still covered in blood. Once the procedure was done, I excused myself and took off the surgical gowns, and washed up.

What I learned from all the surgeries that I scrubbed in on, the emotional exhaustion from the time I start the preoperative instruction to the cutting of the skin, to fixing what needs to be fixed, to closing with the staples or sutures, is that it is like running a marathon. Once you're done, you're exhausted. But in surgery, you have to recollect your thoughts before heading into the next one, and so by the time you're done, it can leave you drained. I don't think the patient fully understands the mental mindset it takes to do this type of work.

Year-end Dinner to Celebrate Our Accomplishments: Here Is My Business Card

At the end of my Residency program, the other two residents and I worked with a Pharmaceutical Representative who would come into the clinic often. He agreed to sponsor a dinner in a high-end restaurant. All the doctors who helped in the residency program showed up with their wives, and we all dressed in nice ties and shirts. I even took a date with me to dinner who would soon be my wife; she did not know it at the time. I handed out my business cards at the dinner to the other doctors and attendings. Most of the doctors were very surprised, one even said, "Well, this is the first, I have never had a resident give me a business card." I had been researching employment opportunities months prior to completing my residency program. I was offered a job in Las Vegas and would be starting my private practice in less than three weeks from the time I graduated from the program.

My Ultimate Goal: Marriage and Starting a Family

My first paycheck from working for another doctor after my residency was less $680. I just told myself that it was only my first week, and it would get better. I had got an apartment close to a house I was having built and was preparing to propose to the girl I met in Arizona. I had to borrow the money to buy the engagement ring. I had everything planned. I flew my girlfriend up to Vegas, had a great dinner at the Bellagio, and watched the O show.

Right after the show, we drove up to see my parents in Utah. Little did she know that I would be asking her for marriage later that night. My brothers were busy putting everything together as I had outlined. The drive was long, and the night was stretching into the early hours of the next day. As I pulled into town, I had to wake her up, being in a daze, her eyes began to widen. I slowly proceeded down the driveway of my parents' home, and lights were strung from one end of the yard to the house that had a message that asked, "Will you marry me?"

In the middle of the light, a dozen red roses hung. I reached down under the seat and grabbed the box with the ring that I had bought and opened it, and asked her to marry me. She said yes. Words could not describe my feelings of excitement after the sweating palms and drenched armpits, and losing more hair from the anxiety of asking.

We married on a very warm fall day in Arizona. The whole family came to celebrate the wedding. My best man was Corona; I had to repay him for having me be his best man at his wedding. Early the next day, we drove up to the Grand Canyon. It had not even been a full day into our marriage when I noticed something that caught my eye, which made me question my decision to marry her. Still, I suppressed it and enjoyed the honeymoon.

I Did Not Expect That! I Want to Go Back to Arizona

Pregnant and stuck in an apartment in a town she was not too familiar with, it started to take a toll on my new bride as I was working long hours in the clinic and on call 24/7 for the first seven months straight. She said she wanted to move back to Arizona. I enjoyed coming home to her after clinic and would love talking to the new one coming into our family. As my voice would reach the belly of my bride, I would notice the activity in the tummy. My words were only positive, and I could not wait to see the child.

I accepted my wife wanting to go back to Arizona, and so I gave my notice to my boss. I had worked so hard to get this job in a very busy clinic, but my family came first. I moved my wife down to Arizona, and I stayed back in Las Vegas for another 4 months to help find my replacement. Plus, I purposely tanked the Arizona State licensing exam the previous summer and had to retake it. I felt it was not necessary to have a license in Arizona when I had a license in Nevada. Money was tight, and every little bit mattered. Staying four months allowed me to work and make a little more, and then retake the state license in June.

When I informed my boss I was leaving his practice, his exact words were: "At least you will be happy in the eternities; you are a better man than I am, sticking with her."

Even though my first experience with private practice did not work out the way I wanted it, my family was my top priority, and I felt I had to go back to Arizona. I met a lot of patients that I still talk about today. One of them was a young teenage boy who came in for warts on his feet. I quit counting after 80 and told him to go home, take some L-lysine, a natural amino acid, and eliminate all sugars from his diet, and if possible, apply silver duct tape and return in three weeks. When the boy returned to the clinic, he did not have a single wart on his foot. I feel that was the first eye-opening experience I had with nutrition in my practice.

Another patient was a person with diabetes who was fascinating to work with; he was a professional baseball player who pitched in the World Series against the Yankees in the 1950s. He would tell me about pitching against some of the greats like Hank Aaron, Joe DiMaggio, Mickey Mantle, Ernie Banks, Willie Mays, Jackie Robinson, and many others. I remember shaking his hand; it was bigger and stronger than a man who milked cows for a living.

Facing the State Board Again in Order to Practice

I moved back to Arizona, but could not practice because I did not have a state license. I stood before the board and tried my best to answer the oral examination questions. There was no time to worry if I did not pass; I had a child on the way and bills to pay. I was told, "Congratulations, you're now licensed in Arizona."

Once I got my license number, I started to apply for all the insurance, which took several months to do. This allowed me time to find a location to practice and help my wife with our new child coming into the world. The main challenge I was facing was getting a bank to loan me some money to start up my practice. Every bank I went to turned me down. After going to six banks, I went back to the one bank that offered me a credit card. That credit card paid for my equipment, supplies, and my employee's salary until I made enough that I could use checks to pay my bills.

The Birth of My First Child: Words Cannot Describe How I Felt

On July 31st, the midwife came to the house to help with the delivery. The baby that everyone thought was for sure going to be a girl came out and was defiantly a boy. I was there for his birth and helped with the delivery. I kind of went into doctor mode, making sure the baby was ok, and my wife was ok. As soon as he was born, and my wife's family filled the little house, I ran off to go and buy some clothes that were blue instead of pink.

Holding Logan for the first time on my chest right after he was born was priceless. I cannot explain the feeling I had of being a father. Having Logan in my life made it difficult to go to work. I just wanted to be there with every smile he made and every step he took as he was going from crawling to walking in a few years.

The hard times did not let up, money was still tight, and I was still trying to keep my practice above water. I would even resort to 5 for 5 Arby's roast beef sandwiches for my birthday dinner, but with the grace of God, we made it through our first year.

Reflection

In the end, my journey taught me that life's hardest detours—failed boards, black ice, gruff attendings, long nights, tight money, and tough choices—are the very roads that shape our courage, deepen our faith, and clarify what matters most. I learned to pray first, show up early, work harder than my doubt, and speak up when my heart said there was more I could give. I learned that humility and curiosity open doors, that pain can become purpose (even saving a life), that respect is earned by consistency, and that the three A's—Availability, Affability, Ability—still win the day. I learned to choose family when careers collide, to keep learning when pride gets bruised, to laugh in cold ORs, and to notice beauty—from sandhill cranes at dawn to the first cry of my son.

If you're facing your own uncertain stretch, take the next right step with grit and grace: pray, prepare, persevere; serve first, trust your gut, ask for help, and let setbacks teach you what strength really feels like. You may not control the storm, but you can steer by faith, love, and disciplined effort—one patient, one decision, one brave "yes" at a time.

CHAPTER 9

The Power of a Promise

All truly wise thoughts have been thought already thousands of times; But to make them truly ours, we must think them over again honestly, Till they take root in our personal experience

— Goethe

I am amazed that when we make a promise to one individual, it also impacts others. My dad would always make a promise to another farmer or client with a handshake. Eleven years prior, I had told Corona I would treat his people in Tonga when I finished Medical School, not knowing the how and when. I shook his hand, and what followed was an adventure that they could make a great movie about.

The Phone Call: Would You Like to Go to Tonga?

When my residency director found out that I was back in Arizona, he reached out to me. He asked if I would be interested in going to Tonga with his church on a medical mission. He showed me the dates. As excited as I was to say yes immediately, I had to talk with my wife. I would be missing clinic for three weeks and, more importantly, I would be missing my boy's first birthday.

After explaining my promise I made to Corona to my wife, she gave her approval. I made the call back: "Count me in." I began working on getting a passport and paying the bills ahead of schedule. I knew it would be a struggle financially; no money would be coming in while I was gone, and I had to pay for everything to go. With the decision made and preparations underway, departure day arrived, carrying me from anticipation to the unknown.

The Island Shaped Like a Shoe: Welcome to Tongatapu

Wednesday, July 25th, 2001: I left for the airport at 11:00 a.m. I finished packing the night before, and my wife and son saw me off at the Phoenix Airport. Logan had a bad cough, and knowing I would be missing his first birthday made it harder to leave. I gave both a hug and a kiss and boarded the plane. The endless water from the view outside the window increased my anxiety. Occasionally, I lifted the cover to the window and peeked. As we passed the equator, I could see little spots of land, then I saw the Island where my best friend was born, it looked like a shoe surrounded by water. As we got closer to the main Island, the water turned from blue to green; I must have gone through one roll of film before we even landed.

Kingdom of Tonga Medical Mission 2001.

While I looked across the vast miles of ocean waters, the young boy that I mentioned in the introduction lay in the hospital bed, thinking, "Can I walk again?" and "Is there anyone here on the island who could help me?" Maybe he was praying for a miracle to happen. Maybe our medical team was his miracle? I will soon know in a few short days.

Stepping off the jet in Tonga.

As I continued to stare out the window, I was asking myself how this big jet was going to land on that small island. As the jet got closer, the ground got wider, and we landed safely. We walked down the long stairs onto the tarmac. I noticed a guard with a German Shepherd dog as we entered this little metal shack that was used for customs. When I heard the people talking in a foreign language, I knew I was here. Greeted by some of the members who were on the medical team, they helped us load our luggage, and off we went to the main greeting place.

As we drove through the countryside, the houses were like you would see in my home of Arizona, with metal roofing, with little to no paint on the houses. I noticed a lot of dogs and pigs running freely in the yards. I asked the driver if there was a speed limit. No sooner than he said yes, a cop came out of the bushes with a radar gun and pulled us over. I said to myself, "Boy, you would think I'm back in Arizona, with cops hiding in the bushes and metal roofs on top of houses."

Arrived at the Parish in Nuku'alofa

Our first day was spent mainly unpacking the large containers of donated items, from school supplies to hospital supplies. We met with one of the main dignitaries of the Island. He said, "I know you are foot doctors here to help my people, but I give you full reign to do whatever you feel comfortable doing in medicine. You have been granted this by my words and the position I hold."

There was a lavish dinner to celebrate our arrival, and the tables were filled with food. Imagine Thanksgiving dinner but with pork, rice, and local fruits and vegetables. My first drink on the island was a fresh coconut. We were told not to drink the water because it would make us sick.

Soane introduced us, but he was speaking in Tonga, so I did not understand a word. As he was introducing me, he got choked up and teary-eyed and pointed to me. One of the ladies who could speak English said you are a special man and that I belonged to the LDS Church, but he is here with us in our Catholic parish. The night was shortened due to a car on the street hitting the power pole, and there were no more lights to see each other to meet and greet. I was shown to the place where I would sleep, which was a bed and a small room. That is all I needed, as I was so exhausted.

The next morning, I woke up and took a shower at 5:00 a.m. It was the coldest shower that I had ever taken. They use the rainwater to shower. I had time to go for a walk, and a member of the team joined me. We walked by the King's palace and along the ocean side. Stopped by the Catholic church, and they were having a bake sale, so I got to eat some desserts. I don't know what it was, but it was good. The team members had to get back to do the Saturday morning masses. I made it to the Catholic mass; boy, they do not let you sleep in church! I don't think I would have been a good Catholic; you're always having to get up and then down the entire service. I was asked if I would like to go to see my temple and church. I said yes, so I went. The nun dropped me off and told me she would be back to pick me up. The temple presidency greeted me. They understood English, which was great. I informed them that I was with the Catholic church, but if any of the members of the LDS church would like to be seen or treated, they could come over to the little clinic at the parish.

Between sacred spaces and sweeping coastlines, the island began to reveal both its beauty and its breath. On the way back to where I was staying, the driver showed me the blowholes. It is the longest chain of blowholes in the world. There were no beaches on this side of the island, just a jagged edge of rocks with these holes that would blow water high in the sky as the tides would come in.

I was asked to join the group for a 16-year-old's birthday party. There were nine covered canopies, and each one had tables with food. We sat at the guest table. The cake was 26 very large pieces. The prayer over the food lasted for half an hour. I did not get to eat half of the items on the table. The entertainment was full of excitement and joy. I observed that the children were very well-mannered and behaved, and respected their parents.

Plan on Going to Prison if You Get in a Car Accident: No Doctors on Call on Weekends

Sunday, I slept in for an extra hour when my alarm went off around 6:30 am. I decided to take a walk after the very short shower experience. As I was walking on the roadside, down to the king's palace, suddenly, two vehicles collided at high speeds. The van had run on a stop sign, and the taxi smashed into the van. I quickly ran over there to help. I asked the driver of the taxi if he was ok, but I don't know if he understood me, as I was speaking English. He was walking around barefoot on the broken glass in a daze. The police quickly came, but there was no ambulance. They placed the man wandering around in the police car, and then the man inside the van was stuck.

Some of the people from the village came running out with their garden tools and started to pry open the door. The man's face was bleeding severely, and blood was coming out of his mouth. I asked if they were going to the hospital and introduced myself as a doctor from the States. They said, "No, no, no doctor!"

I later found out they both took them to the local prison and waited until Monday to take them to the hospitals. I also learned that the doctor at the hospital only works Monday through Friday, and there are no on-call doctors. That explains why they did not go directly to the hospital, and it explained to me why we had not been to the hospital to start work when we arrived on the Island.

Church with No Piano: Only a Heavenly Choir to Listen to

I spent the rest of the day going to my church. Two of the nuns took me to my church and made sure I found the place to worship. I was greeted with smiles and hugs. They all made me feel like I was part of their family. I noticed there were no pianos; they did not need them. Their voices were like angels from a heavenly choir.

As I sat there not understanding an ounce of what was being said, I just enjoyed the strong spirit that filled the room. Occasionally, I noticed that as soon as the children were disruptive, they were immediately taken out. Maybe my mom was part Tongan? "She would do the same thing to me when I grew restless in church." The windows to the building are opened for the cool breeze. I was invited to eat with some members. They had a very humble place; they laid a plastic tarp on the living room floor and placed the main course on it. Then we sat on the floor and ate.

As soon as I made it back to the parish, I was informed of our schedule tomorrow; it looks like we will be doing hospital rounds and surgery all day.

Some Wrapped Packages You Just Don't Want to Open

For the past two mornings, I could not understand the loud thumping sounds outside. I walked to the sounds of the thump and noticed these chickens falling out of the large Ficus tree. I don't know if they woke up during the fall or woke up after hitting the ground. But it was the funniest thing to watch. I did get my morning walk in the darkness of the morning sky; the stars seem so close that you could pick one like an apple off a tree.

The medical team met up and went to the hospital. We met with the director of the hospital to show us the only hospital on the Island; it was like a mash unit.

Hospital at the capital city of Tonga in Nuku'alofa.

While making our way to each of the patient rooms, I noticed a person following behind us. They patiently waited outside each room as we went from room to room. I asked the interpreter if she could ask the individual who was following us if they needed something. We stopped, and the interpreter learned of a little boy who needed our help, and if it was possible to see him. We said yes and made our way to his room once we finished seeing all the patients on the list.

As we walked into the little boy's room, we were greeted by his mom and dad. I noticed the child was in a lot of pain as he lay on his left side; his right foot and leg were completely bandaged all the way up to his knee. I tried to remove the dressing, but it was too painful. I asked what had happened, and they told us that he was playing with his cousin and was hit by a car and drug down the driveway along the gravel path. They rushed him to the hospital, but all they could do for the past few days was pray to God that something could help our child. We informed the parents that we would put him on the schedule for surgery at 1:30 p.m. We had no idea what we were about to uncover.

Right after seeing all the patients on the list and the little boy, we went on our general surgery rounds. We were shown a 9-year-old girl with possible osteomyelitis, a 6-month-old with clubfoot, an 8-year-old with clubfoot and a 17-year-old with clubfoot, and a sumo wrestler with a badly infected big toe. They were all on our schedule for surgery.

Constraints were everywhere—scarcity shaping every decision.

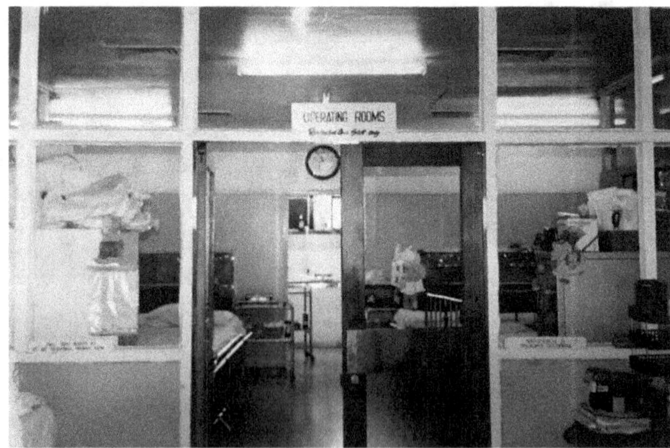

Operating room in the hospital in Nuku'alofa.

We were told we only had one mask per day, so make it last. The water they used for flushing in surgery came out of the sink down the hallway.

Our first surgery was on a 6-month-old baby with club feet. Our second surgery was for a 7-year-old boy with severe foot deformity. He had previous surgery and some of his bones in his feet were missing; the talus was in a vertical position (a position not too common). We were able to fuse a few bones together. After this procedure, and during our break between our next surgical case, I went back to the hospital floor and saw around six to seven patients. I went back into surgery, and we then worked on the 17-year-old boy with severe right foot deformity. It took us about 4 and half hours to complete. There was a lot of bleeding. The sumo wrestler we also took into surgery to remove the tip of his toe as he had an infection in the bone.

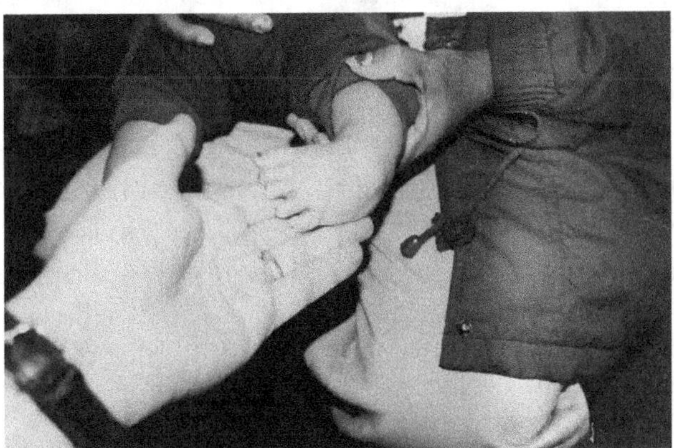

6th month old child with clubfoot.

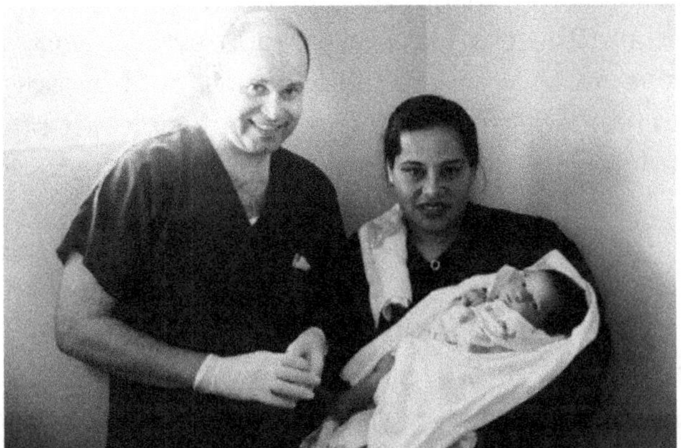

6th month old child with clubfoot and mother.

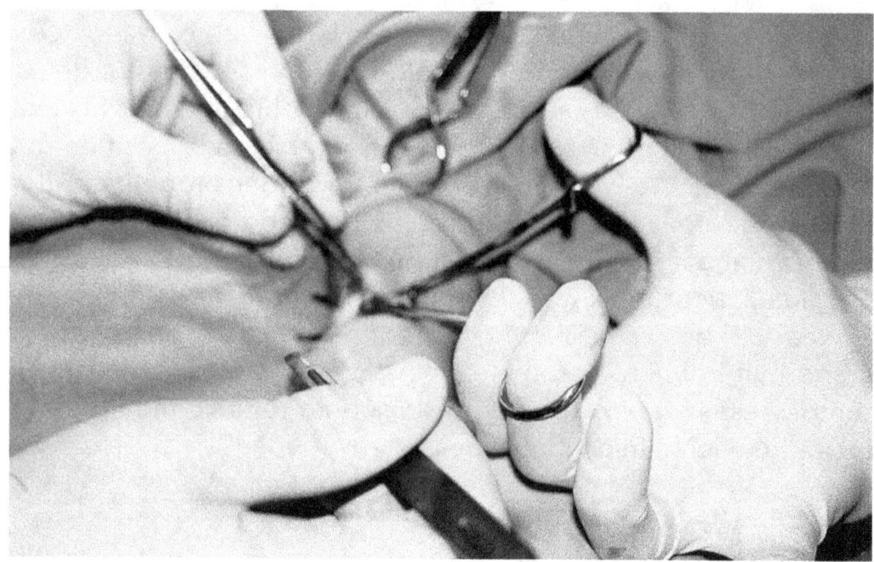

In surgery on the 6th month old child for club foot.

I learned from the medical staff that if you are transported to the hospital by ambulance, the only person with you is the driver, and staying the night in the hospital is $1. People wait four to six hours to be seen by a doctor and don't even complain. If you go on the weekend, you're going to have to wait until Monday for a doctor to see you.

We finally got to the child who was hit by the car. We were running late, but we still took him into surgery. As the parents were stopped at the door and the child lay on the gurney and was moved into the Operative room, we were ready to find out how severe his leg was under all those bandages. The anesthesiologist on our medical team sedated the child, then we unwrapped the bandages.

It was a good thing I developed a strong stomach in surgery over the years, as when we took off the dressing, half of the leg was gone, and the top of his foot was gone. The top of the child's foot was exposed bone; all you could see was gravel and dark tissue, and exposed bones from the tip of his toes up to his knees. Our first goal was to identify if the leg was worth saving, because the longer this went exposed, the risk was higher for the child to develop sepsis and could die. We took out the gravel from the exposed bones and joints and used the sink water to flush the leg and foot. The little toe was dangling and black as the night sky; it had to be removed. Once all the tissue was cleaned, we then inspected each bone that was exposed, and we could see there was still good blood flow to the bones. We decided to try to save the child's leg.

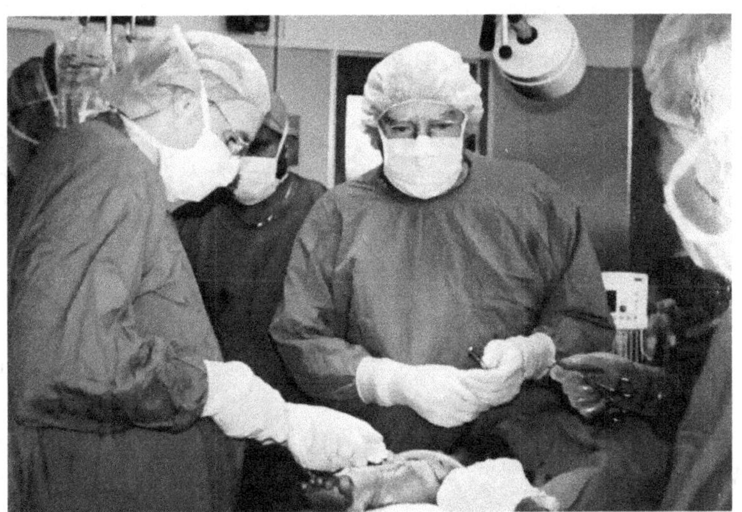

Dr Robison and Dr Reese making a decision on the child to save his leg in the operative room.

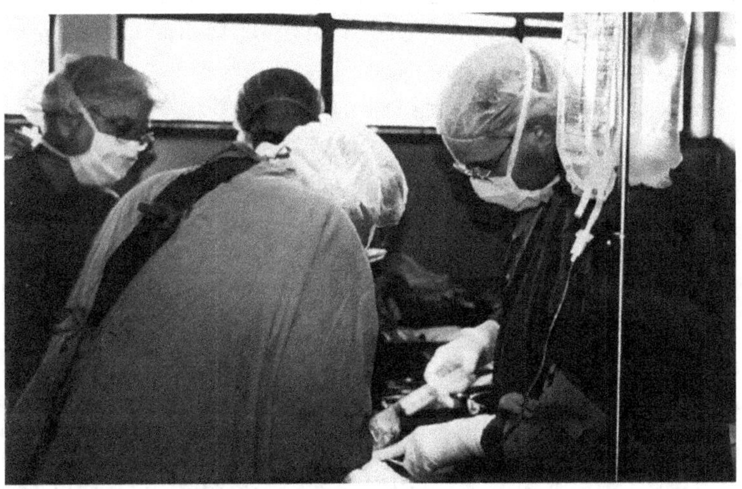

Dr Robison and Dr Reese performing surgery on a child to save his leg.

The main lingering question was: how in the world are we going to close such a large area of body surface? It would have been so easy to amputate the leg. Still, there were no braces and prosthetics on the island. That child would be given a tree branch made into a crutch and would have to walk around the rest of his life like that if he remained on the island. Amputation was not in our treatment plan; we were determined to find a way to cover the area. Skin grafts were not an option; the area to close was too large. We decided to approach the OB-GYN department and ask them for a placenta from a newborn baby. That was not an option as there were no newborns, and secondly, taking tissue from a newborn was not heard of on the island, and more than likely, the mother would not approve of such a thing for religious purposes, but it was a good idea.

We put a dressing back on his leg to help the tissue stay moist and keep it from drying out. We then decided to call in a general surgery and proposed an idea that would require the general surgeon to be involved after we left the island, because we were only there for just a little over two weeks.

He was all ears, so we proposed to him that we would open his good leg by making an incision on the back side from the knee down into the foot, creating a natural skin flap to be sutured on top of the damaged leg and foot. The child would have to remain on his back or in a sitting position. The entire time, the child could not walk, and this may take months to know if it was even working, as you would be required to remove a suture or two each week. It would have to be up to you, as the general surgeon, to make that call.

He said, "I like your idea; let's do it." There were a lot of risk factors, infections, abscesses, damaged and nonfunctioning tendons to help him walk, and unforeseen complications. This was a procedure that required much faith, hope, and prayer. It was now truly in God's hands and the medical team that remained on the island. Only time would tell if that child would ever walk again.

Leprosy: I Thought It Was Only Found in the Bible

The first thing I did today was make a call back home to wish my boy Logan a happy birthday. It was the one thing that I questioned most about going. It was his 1ˢᵗ birthday, and I wanted so badly to be there with him, celebrating his birthday, watching him play in the cake, opening his presents, and then giving him a big hug and kiss on the cheek. As I listened to the phone ring, it went to voicemail. All I could do was leave a message, wishing him a happy birthday.

I did not have time to call again, as I was off to the leper colonies. Mayla accompanied me. Most of the lepers were not in an active state. Those who had active leprosy were flown over to Fiji for treatment. We were there to help with the sores and foot deformities that developed because of leprosy.

I learned that the first area we went to was called the lowlands, which is a place where trash was dropped from households, hotels, and businesses. When the high tide came in, it would push the deposited garbage into this area, and people would have to walk through the knee-high waters to get to their houses that were on stilts. They would contract leprosy, elephantiasis, and other parasitic diseases from the contaminated waters.

It just happened to be a low tide when we were there. The one lady that I was asked to see had leprosy, and her foot became very deformed in the process. Now she was being treated for an ulceration on her foot.

The next patient we saw was a man who was lying on his back on a wooden bed. I asked the interpreter if he could roll over so I could assess the ulceration on his back, as he painfully turned to the side, literally thousands. I mean, thousands of maggots fell off his back and onto the bed. His entire back was one big open sore. I told the interpreter to have him lie back down. The maggots kept his wound clean, but I did not know how much longer he would survive. I recommended he go to the hospital for better care.

Home visits of a leprosy patient.

Tongan Dinners and the Triage That Followed

Every evening, the Catholic Church would put on these special dinners for our group in various communities throughout the week. This evening, we went to a small village where the blowholes were. The driver of the car asked if I would like to drive the car over to see the blowholes before the dinner began. I did; it was weird driving on the wrong side of the road. I spent a few minutes watching the waves coming in and then watching the miles and miles of water being shot up into the air. It was one of the most spectacular things that I have seen in nature. After dinner, we examined the people to see who needed to be seen in the clinic and who needed to be seen in the hospital. This went on into the early hours of the next day.

Eleven Years Later: The Promise Was Fulfilled

The next morning, I got up an hour earlier at 4:30 a.m. to go to the LDS temple. One of the nuns took me to the temple and had me picked up to go to the clinic after I was done. As I was leaving the temple, the man at the temple asked me to see his wife, then his 1st counselor, and then his secretary. They wanted me to go to the local LDS Center close by to treat the members of their church. I declined the requests and offered the invitation to anyone who would like to see me; they could come over to the Catholic parish clinic, and I would gladly see them. I felt it was only right for me to stay with the Catholic church as I was a part of their medical team. A few of those that I treated in the Temple that morning were a direct relative of Corona. I had truly fulfilled my promise to him.

After changing into my scrubs, I went to the clinic at the Catholic parish where they had a small clinic where I worked with Sister Joan. She oversaw the little clinic in her parish. Once word got out that there was an American doctor on the Island, the line to be seen got very long. All the medical training in South Dakota really helped; I felt comfortable examining from head to toe and treating all sorts of conditions that came into the clinic. It did not scare me to see someone in the clinic with a knee condition, shoulder, and arm conditions, and even elephantiasis, ringworm, and sickle cell anemia.

One of the last patients of the morning was a little girl who needed to have a growth removed from her foot. With limited anesthesia, I could see the patient in pain, but she just remained in the exam chair and did not say a word as I removed the growth. Some of the patients were so grateful that they left money. I said thank you and gave it to Sister Joan. I loved helping people, and some thoughts did cross my mind about being a family doctor, but I loved my profession, and so these thoughts were short-lived. The easiest way to break those thoughts was to think about basic science and having to retake the Medical National Boards Part I all over again.

That afternoon, we went to a Baptist high school. There were about 1,200 students who attended there. They all sat on the floor, with the boys on one side and the girls on the other side. They were some of the most respectful children that I had seen. When they handed out the food and drinks, I ate the good food, but then I realized that after drinking from the cup that was handed to me, it was water. When I asked what was in the cup, they said water. Well, we will see how well my stomach can handle whatever I just drank.

Montezuma Revenge: I Warned You Not to Drink the Water

The next morning, I had severe diarrhea. I had a lot of stomach pain, thinking it might have been the octopus that I ate, but more than likely it was from the water I drank. I went back to the clinic while Dr Reese stayed at the hospital and did the surgeries. In the clinic, it was like being a family doctor, kind of like when I helped with the clinic in South Dakota and the boys' and girls' camp. I saw gallbladder issues, scabies, allergic reactions, and hay fever. I injected the hips and knees, and feet. I even removed a suspicious mole on a lady's face that was very suspicious of cancer. I removed two of the moles and sutured her face back up.

I was asked to go back to the hospital and help with surgery on a patient who had a surfing accident. Surfing in Tonga is extreme, as there are no real beaches, just rows and rows of jagged rocks. I was informed that this surfer's ankle was pointed in the opposite direction after hitting the rocks. It was also the day that the medical team was to fly over to the Island of Eua. After talking to Dr Reese, we felt that it was best for me to go ahead to the airport and catch the flight over to this small island. Dr Reese would later fly over with the rest of the team after the surgery was complete.

Island of Eua: Your Hand Does Not Look Normal

The Island of Eua had a population of 4,000. A lot of people were sick, medication was limited, and antibiotics were very hard to get.

It was a good thing that I left early for the airport, as the flight was half an hour early. Dr Reese and his wife missed the flight and would have to take a flight the next day. That means I was on my own to handle the clinic. The trip was a 7-minute flight. The runway was small, and we landed safely.

The doctor on the island took me to the village where I would be staying for a few days. They had sleeping bags laid out on the floor of a large room. By this time, it did not matter to me where I slept, just as long as I got a few hours to sleep. All I was concerned about was having a toilet nearby in case of diarrhea. I notice a group of men on the opposite side of the room sitting down with their legs folded underneath each other, smoking "Kava," the Tongan version of Marijuana. It was a stimulant. Still, by just seeing them sit there, I realized why some of those patients in the clinic came in with sores and ulceration on their outer ankle bones.

I was asked to see my first patient upon arriving. It was a lady who a child bit in her class on the finger, and now her wrist was the size of a grapefruit. Her finger was necrotic and needed attention. While waiting for the instruments to be sterilized, I was asked to join the Kava party by the island doctor as I sat there with the doctor and the men of the island. I was offered to try some Kava but kindly declined, and they respected that. One of the men in the group knew the Corona family.

Around 9 p.m., I went back to the Hospital to perform the surgery. The doctor stayed behind with his buddies at the kava party.

I took the patient into the operative room. The room was filled with flies. I asked to open the windows to help remove some of the flies before I did the incision and drainage on the patient's hand. They handed me a bar of soap and pointed me to the sink in the prep area to get ready for surgery.

I then asked for the instrument tray that they had sterilized. I opened it, and it was fully rusted. All I knew was that I could not use their instruments. Luckily, I had my medical bag and pulled out a scalpel and surgical blade. I used some local anesthetic that they had and did my best to numb up the infected wrist and finger.

I have found that when you're dealing with an infection, you need more local anesthetics to numb a digit. I prepped the finger and wrist the best I could, and once the wrist and finger were numb. I proceeded to make an incision over the finger, and pus came shooting out. I then started to lengthen the incision down to the wrist, with more pus coming out of the infected area. I asked for a culture kit, but they informed me they did not have anything that was used for culturing to know what antibiotics to use. I cleaned up most of what I could and flushed it with sink water, bandaged it up, and recommended she catch the next available flight to the main Island to help save her hand.

Exhausted by the excitement of the event and the diarrhea, I did not stay with the men at the kava party. Still, I took the one antibiotic I had brought with me and found a sleeping bag, and fell asleep.

Island of Eua sleeping quarters.

It Was Not Right That I Was the Last Thing He Saw

Words are difficult to describe these days, because of what happened. I was asked to stop by a man's house on my way to the clinic. He was in respiratory distress. I listened to his heart with my stethoscope and said it would be best to have him come to the clinic to receive some oxygen. I left his house; I could see in his eyes that I was his last hope for medical attention.

I even asked for an inhaler to help him breathe, but since medication was in short supply, I could not even get that for him. When I arrived at the hospital, the man that I had seen at his house had arrived at the hospital in respiratory distress. The island doctor started an IV and got the oxygen tank when he realized there was none in the tank. The entire island had no oxygen. The patient was having more difficulty breathing, and was getting worse, the Island doctor pushed some dopamine into the IV and then atropine. The patient coded on me; I started CPR with breathing, along with chest compressions. I did not know how long I was performing CPR on him as he would come in and out of consciousness. He opened his eyes and looked at me, then closed his eyes, and he was gone. I quickly switched from giving him breaths to heart compression, and I even heard a rib crack. At one point, the doctor was trying to intubate him, but what good would that have done since there was no oxygen for him?

At this point, I could not bring him back. The emotions took over me; I had never had a person die in my arms. The patient just lay there on the table with the sheet over his body. The island doctor said, "I am going home; you're in charge," and left. I was left in the room alone with the patient, I found a corner of the room and put my head down and just wept as I sat there with tears rolling down my face, going over everything in my mind of what I could have done different, it was not right for me to be the last person this patient saw, he trusted me with his life. He had hope that an American doctor could fix him. After beating myself up for a short time, I knew we had patients to see as the line of patients was getting longer outside the clinic.

I later realized that for the past year, there was no doctor on the island. And if someone came in with Congestive Heart Failure, they would place them on a bed and let them die. I did not blame God. His miracles are real, but he needs us as much as we need him. We are his hands on earth. Yes, he performs miracles every single day; some we don't see or hear about. My life is filled with miracles. I will always give thanks to God for placing me in his place to offer my helping hand.

One of the medical staff members came over and placed her hand on my shoulder and hugged me. She knew it was difficult for me, but she asked, "Are you ready to see the patients?" There were 49 patients lined up to be seen, with more on their way. With the island doctor gone for the day, I could not take any more of the precious time by feeling sad, so we went to work to see as many patients as we could.

After working on adrenaline and not stopping for lunch or breaks, and noticing the medical team feeling exhausted, I told one of the staff to let the people know that we would be leaving soon and to come back tomorrow. I asked one of the medical staff if they knew of a place we could go and see the beauty of the island. He confirmed that he knew of the perfect place, and we all went down to the beach. He showed me how to make a hat out of the palm leaves. The medical staff just put their feet in the ocean waters and felt the sand roll over their toes as the waves came in. I sat there watching a fisherman catch an octopus with a spear. It was as if medical life did not exist. I really don't know how long we were there. It was the one time in my life that time did not exist.

Sunday attire for church services on Eua.

Heading back to the place where we were staying, the father of the parish asked if I wanted to take a hot shower. My eyes got big, and I said absolutely. He took me over to his residence, and I got to take a nice warm shower for the first time since being in Tonga. Later that night, we had dinner at the local church. A child came up to me and said, "Hey doc," pointing to his six toes on each foot. "Can you fix this?" Given the island and the medical situation on the island, I don't know if he ever got those toes fixed.

Sunday Morning in Eua: "Why Is Everyone Lining up to See Me?"

Dr Reese and his wife made it to the island, and we took a group photo. Learning what had happened the day before, I was asked if I would like to go and spend time with my church, and I gladly accepted the offer. The rest of the medical team had their services and then went back to the clinic to finish seeing the remaining patients who wanted to be seen.

A Catholic man drove me to church. I had just given away my white shirt, pens, and pencils to the local bishop. Then one of the leaders of the church said, "We need to go to a different church." He drove me over to his church. They were very friendly and very welcoming. I felt out of place because I did not have a white shirt; I had just given it away, as I thought it was my last Sunday there. I would give what I had to the people.

When I arrived at this congregation, they had me stand up and give my testimony of Jesus Christ to the people. It was different because I had to speak so the interpreter could tell the congregation what I was saying in English. I gave thanks to my good friend Corona Ngatuvai for his friendship, his kind heart, as he was the reason why I was with them today. He is my brother, just from a different mother. I made a promise to him that I would treat his people 11 years ago, and here I am. I realized everyone in Tonga is family, and when you treat one, you have treated the entire family of Tonga.

Once I was done, the church leader stood up and said in his native tongue, "Now there is an American doctor here, so any one of you who needs to be seen, meet him after church." All the people in the congregation's eyes got big. "So, anyone who would like to be seen, just meet us here after church."

I thought I got out of the clinic by going to church, but I had my own clinic and made do with what little I had. In a way, it was like Jesus feeding the thousand with five loaves of bread and fish. It seemed as if my supplies in my medical bag lasted until the last patient. I guess the greatest gift I could give was some form of treatment, and a smile to say that there is always hope in this world.

After all the patients were seen, the church leader took me over to a church member at Hideaway resorts, who cooked me rice and fish. It felt good on my stomach. Then another church member took me in his Land Rover to see more patients.

I met a man who could not walk. Then I saw his wife, and he later took me to a man with a tooth extraction. Talk about treating from head to toe! I was asked to go and see an entire family. He then drove me from one side of the island to the other side. Boy, what a short ride.

Later that night, I met up with President Finau, the leader of the LDS church and the Catholic church children's choir. I was asked to say a few words, and I must have said something right as they clapped.

There was a little girl named Anna who was only five years old. Her father had died, and I don't know what happened to her mother. I was told she was being raised by her relatives. If I had room in my pocket, I could have taken her home with me. She just followed me around all night. Children are so precious; I don't know how anyone could hurt them. I finally fell asleep at 12:00 a.m.

Tongan Trench: Hold on Tight, the Ride of My Life

Instead of flying back to the main Island, we caught a ferry boat at 3:30 a.m. to save money. My diarrhea did not stop. Right before getting on the boat, I had to go so badly, I was even looking for the nearest tree. I found an old outhouse that had some plywood boards with a small hole. It had to be the most disgusting place that I had ever had a bowel movement. It smelled so bad; it was even worse than a nursing home urine smell. Luckily, I had some toilet paper with me. It was a miracle that I did not fall into the depths of human waste. I was better off going behind a tree. I boarded the boat at 4:45 a.m. They told me to go up on top of the ferry boat, and I would not get as sick going through the Tongan trench, the deepest parts of the Pacific Ocean, and even on a good day, the waters were fierce.

Outhouse used for my bout of diarrhea.

I found my place at the highest point on the boat and held on to the ropes for dear life as the waves began to hit the boat, and my face was being splashed with saltwater. The boat was going sideways and up and down; it was a good thing that I let go of my insides before boarding, or it would have been a much different experience. All I could do was think about my father as he sailed over to Korea to fight in the war. I wonder how he felt when he was on the ship for all those days on the water. I swore to myself that if I got off the boat safely, I would not go back on the open ocean again. As we approached the main island, I pried my white-knuckle fingers off the rope and stood up. The last ten minutes, I stared at the land in the distance as we came into the Island.

As soon as I came off the boat, I went and had an X-ray on my thumb, only to find out it was broken in two places. I did not record how I broke my thumb, but it was hurting and very tender. Once I bandaged my thumb, I went back to the clinic to help patients. A patient came in with 90 percent burns over her legs from an accident when hot water splashed on her legs. I immediately sent her over to the hospital. It will be nice to sleep in a bed, I wrote in my journal. I finally talked to my wife; it was the most beautiful voice on the trip. Everything is fine back home; I wish I could get over the diarrhea. I was up all night with diarrhea, but managed to get the strength to go to the clinic. There were a lot of people lined up to be seen.

For lunch, the hospital took us all out to a cafe. I did not order anything as my stomach was still hurting. One of the medical staff members did not like what she had ordered. It was rude not to eat what was placed in front of you, "I know every time Corona had me over for dinner, I ate what was placed in front of me, and his mom would rub the side of my ribs and say Boy, you need to eat more, you're too skinny." That is why I never ordered; I just felt that if I ordered something, then I had to rush to the bathroom, and that would be rude. As she pushed her dish to the side, I took her dish and placed it in front of me so it would not show any disrespect. I started to eat it when I was told that it was a shellfish to which I was highly allergic. I was advised after my near-death experience not to eat any shellfish as it had the same ingredients as the contrast dye that caused my anaphylactic reaction. No sooner than I realized what I had done, my throat started to tighten and tingle, and my breathing was becoming more difficult.

Without making a scene, I quietly asked one of the medical team members if they had any Benadryl. He did and pulled one out of his bag. I excused myself and went to the restroom and popped it in my mouth, and swallowed, praying this would stop the reaction that was starting to happen. I went back to the dining table and took my place, and waited for the remaining speeches to finish. It felt like an eternity, as soon as the last speaker was done, the group was planning on taking the rest of the day off and would spend it at the beach. I asked if someone could take me to the hospital and explained why. They quickly took me to the hospital and dropped me off at the emergency room. The medical staff quickly took me in and began to monitor my breathing. Instead of giving me the EPI shot, they just laid me in one of the hospital beds and watched me for a few hours.

While the medical team was enjoying the beach, I was looking outside the one window, imagining myself at the beach. I was thankful to the medical staff who were monitoring my condition. Boy, every day is a story to tell here in Tonga. I am trying to figure out why my tongue is completely black. It must have come from the shellfish that I ate.

My Last Patients Seen Were in Prison

I was asked to go to the prison right before the big farewell party, with a few of the medical team. We arrived at the Prison, and I noticed the prisoners were dressed in T-shirts, and they were draped in blue. There were no handcuffs, no chairs, and the prisoners were driving the vehicle. It makes sense; I mean, where would they go if they tried to escape from the prison? The entrance gate was a checkpoint, but it appeared to be unarmed, even though many had been there for years for their crimes.

I was asked to speak to the prisoners. The first thing that came to mind was a scripture that said, "Ye I know I am nothing as to my strength I am weak for I will not boast of myself, but I will boast of my God for in his strengths I can do all things."

One of the patients I saw in the prison was doing time for burglary. He was touched by what I said. I treated him.

Treated prisoners just hours before leaving Tonga.

Going Away Party from the People of Tonga

After returning from the prison, the big going away party for the medical team with all the furnishing of the island food and the performances from the entertainers were almost over, I managed to eat two bowls of rice. The main question that the people asked me was whether I would be coming back. I just smiled without saying a word. I loved the people, but the cold shower, the toilets, the boat ride, and not having the supplies in the clinic to properly treat patients gave me mixed feelings. Diabetics are still non-compliant; patients are demanding to be seen. And the last six days of diarrhea have been miserable.

I did not like saying goodbye, so I just hanged back in the very back of the room and allowed the people to hug and kiss the cheeks of the medical staff. As I was working my way out of the event, a patient whom I had seen in the Catholic parish with Sister Joan had stopped me and handed me a plaque that was handmade and painted. It said: *Dr Glen Robinson, with sincere appreciation for your medical care in the Kingdom of Tonga, in the year 2001, from your patient.*

I wanted to cry, but I held it in. It was a gift I was not deserving of, and I could tell some of the members of the group were a little jealous. Making comments like I have been here two years, and I have never received something like that. I did not let that bother me. I was thankful for my handmade gift and held this gift as one of the most precious things that I have been given.

Handmade gift given to me of a patient I treated in the clinic.

We loaded up in the vehicles, and they took us to the airport. As we boarded the plane, it started to rain for the first time since we got there. One of the Tongans who saw us off at the airport said the heavens are crying to see you go. As we flew back home, I felt I had left something and realized, yes, I had left a lot of emotions on the island with everyone I helped, to everyone I wished I had more time to help. My thoughts and emotions truly changed my life. If everyone could be like the people of Tonga, there would be no wars, there would be less contention, and there would be more love and peace. They are the most Christ-like people that I have ever met.

The long flight back home gave me ample time to reflect on the promise I made to Corona eleven years ago, and how grateful I was to fulfill this promise. It made me realize that a promise is more powerful than the words themselves; it is a binding force that changes the future for stories to be written about and shared in our history books.

Reflection

In the end, this journey is a testament to the power of a promise kept, the quiet heroism of showing up, and the sacredness of serving with whatever is in your hands—whether it's scarce supplies, a broken thumb, or a heart stretched thin by loss and love. It teaches that resilience is born where scarcity meets creativity, that faith is not passive but practiced in small, steady acts, and that compassion is the bridge between our limitations and another's need. We learn to travel light—open hands, sturdy hearts, curious mind, willing feet—ready to listen, to improvise, to love people more than our comfort, and to keep moving forward even when the seas rise, or the answers run out.

If you remember anything, let it be this: promises shape futures, kindness multiplies in the margins, and hope is built by ordinary people doing the next right thing with extraordinary heart.

CHAPTER 10

The Most Pivotal Time of My Career

Life begins at the end of your comfort zone.

— Neale Donald Walsch

I had not been home for but a few weeks when I was woken up by a phone call from a friend of mine who came to see me. "Have you seen the news?" he asked. I turned on the television only to see the second plane hit the Twin Towers. He was flying back that morning, but all the airports were canceled. I told them to get their things together, and I would drive them back up to Utah. It was a 9-hour drive to meet up with his family. I canceled my clinic and made the drive, being on the road for a total of 18 hours made for a long day. September 11th changed the world. The drive home, I noticed nobody on the roads, and for the next several days, the country was stunned, and everyone was glued to the television set. It literally put the whole country to a stop.

I noticed my patients were more anxious and apprehensive in the clinic. But I also saw the spirit of America come to life. The people were more patriotic.

My clinical practice was growing little by little, and I was doing more and more surgeries in the hospital. I continued to build up the practice, seeing patients of all ages. I was doing everything that I was taught in school. As my practice grew, so did my waist-line. I was eager to take the drug reps' lunches and would go out to a fast-food restaurant to grab a quick bite to eat before going back to the clinic in the afternoon.

The problems with my lower back started to creep in, the seden-tary lifestyle, being overweight, and the stress of life with limited money flowing in, and living next to the mother-in-law really did not help matters either.

With my back pains getting worse, my wife introduced me to a man whom she had been seeing. She said he can help you, as surgery was not an option for me. I had no insurance, and being in private practice for myself, I could not afford the time to take off work to have the back surgery. I agreed to meet this man in Phoenix. What he did to me was the most unconventional form of treatment that I had ever experience, but I was so thankful to him because it worked.

With my wife pregnant with our second child, I was trying to spend as much time with Logan, and most of our dinners were spent at the local Mexican restaurants. Though when she had time to cook, it was very good.

Update on the Young Boy in Tonga

I got a phone call from my residency director asking me if I wanted to go back to Tonga in the late summer. I informed him that I had to pass this year. I did not want to leave my pregnant wife and soon-to-be two-year-old son.

When the medical team came back, I received a call. Dr Reese asked, "Do you remember the little boy with half of his leg gone? Let me give you an update on his status." I often wondered what happened to him. He said the medical team was all in the initial meeting, getting instructions, when the doors at the back of the room flew open and the little boy came running in. His family had heard the medical team was back, and they wanted to come to say thank you. This brought a big smile to my face and made me realize the importance of hope, faith, and prayers in the healing process. This truly was a miracle.

Can Someone Help Me?

I was settled into my new office, the doctor I was sharing rent with moved out of the area, and I could not afford to pay rent for the entire place. I found a place in a new building for a primary care doctor, and he had more rooms than he was using and offered space to put my practice.

One day, while I was working in the clinic, one of the staff personnel from the transport vehicle came into the clinic asking for help for her paraplegic patient, who was seeing the primary doctor. He was in a wheelchair and had not been properly secured in the vehicle. As the vehicle started to leave, he fell. The transport person looked back only to see this man out of his wheelchair, and his neck and head were pinched up against the side of the van, and unable to move. They stopped the vehicle and tried to move him, but they could not move the man, so they rushed back into the clinic to ask for help. I happened to be the only one available.

I went into the van, saw the patient's head and neck pinned up against the wall of the van. I put both of my arms in his armpit and picked him up, not realizing he was 250 pounds. It was a pure adrenaline experience. I soon realized the effect it had on my upper back, as my fingers were now tingling. I had injured my lower back while fighting fires, and I suffered the pains running down my legs, and now I have pain running down my fingers.

I knew I had to go back and see the man who had worked on me before. It had been over a year since I had seen him. I was told by the man helping me to change my eating habits. Working on you is like working on a bag of potatoes. I did not take to heart what he was saying when I first met him. I experienced a part of the stretch that was done to my lower back, but now it was being performed to my upper back and neck.

I wish I could say I changed my eating habits, but I didn't. I started to look like the Pillsbury Dough Boy in my blue scrubs, and I didn't even need the blanket heater. As I got heavier and heavier, my back got sore and sore.

What Just Happened Was the Pivotal Point in My Career

Jesa'Lyn was also born at home with the midwife. Her head was jet black, and she was like this little porcelain doll. She caused me to smile from ear to ear just seeing her bubbly personality. As she was starting to walk, she would come running up to me as I did to my mom, and she would almost knock me over when she jumped into my arms. I loved coming home, seeing her dark brown eyes; she would light up the house. I continued to take Logan with me everywhere; he was like a piece of Velcro stuck to my pant leg, which I truly loved, but Jesa'Lyn was a daddy girl.

When Jesa'Lyn was about two and a half years old, she stopped eating. We really don't know why. We took her to the ER and to the pediatrician with the same answer of a shrugged shoulder, and the only advice was to try something soft to give her. Here I was, an educated doctor who went through medical school, went through a residency program, had my own private practice, and I could not help my daughter. This was beyond feeling frustrated. I was running out of options, so I finally resorted to calling up the man who worked on my lower back. He told me to bring her down. I put my frail little girl into her car seat and made the hour-and-a-half drive.

Upon arrival, I carried my daughter into his office and placed her on the exam table. He looked at her, then did some familiar releases that he had done on me, but in a more precise way. I heard some popping sounds followed by the gurgle sound in her tummy, and then my daughter stood up on the table and said, "Daddy, I am hungry." We took her into the kitchen area and gave her some soft food; she did not have any pain when she ate.

I looked at this man and asked, "What you just did for my daughter, I have to learn. Would you teach me?" He replied, "I will teach you anything."

I had never seen anything like this in my schooling and training. Even though I had been working on myself in the past and experienced the benefits, it was not until Jesa'Lyn's helpless eyes and the man's miracle hands changed my course in how I treated patients.

The first thing I did was follow the recommendation on what I eat. Secondly, I invested my time and money in learning this new way of healing people over the next 18 years. Was it hard for me to make the transition? Yes. For one, I had to eat differently. I had to take the time to learn the material. The more I learned, the more I realized the potential of what was possible. I started to do less surgery in the hospitals and really started to apply the principles in my practice. Nobody could relate to me in my field, so I did not talk much about what I was learning.

Now that I have really invested in this line of work, I trust the process of having my upper body worked on. The first time I got the good release in my upper body, all the events of my childhood head traumas stayed on the table. I could not move my neck for about a week, and my mentor would have fun with it. He would ask me a question, and I would move my whole body towards him to give my reply. I had this newfound freedom that I had not experienced in years.

There was another time in an MRI facility when one of the technicians came running into my clinic asking for help. I went to see the cause of the panic. I noticed a technician. He was pinned up against the MRI machine with the patient's wheelchair. He had gone too close to the machine, and the magnetic force sucked the wheelchair and pinned him behind it. Yes, they could have shut the machine down, but it would have cost $150,000 a day to reboot it. I jumped in and pushed everyone away and got down on the floor, and with my legs up against the machine, I pulled the wheelchair off enough to allow the technician to squeeze out.

When I let go of the wheelchair, I immediately had shooting pains down my legs.

I called up the man who had helped me before. I was invited to his clinic, and he got me out of trouble again. The owner of the building called me up and asked, "How did you take the wheelchair off?" I told him, "We had to drill a hole in the floor and use a come-along to pry it off."

You Can Have Your Femur Broken, or You Can Let Me Do This

One of the techniques I learned was identifying when a hip is caught, what to look for, and then finding out the three sources that could be the reason.

Jesa'Lyn frequently would have her hip worked on by my mentor. I wanted to learn this technique, so I observed it many times before I decided to try it on Jesa'Lyn. I asked her if she would let me work on her, and she said yes, Dad. I laid her on the table just like my mentor would do and then positioned her leg and released her hip. I literally thought I broke her bone from the sounds of the release. She got up, gave me a big hug, and went on playing.

In the clinic, a mother brought her 4-year-old girl into my office. I noticed when she walked down the hallway, one foot was straight forward, and one foot was pointed at a ninety-degree angle. As I placed her on the exam chair, I explained to her mother that I wanted to check the child's hip to see if it was properly tracking. I noticed the leg that was at ninety degrees did not release like the other leg did. I told her you have three choices. First choice: do nothing, which I did not recommend. Second, you could have the femur broken and surgical reposition, which they usually do when the child is at this age. Or lastly, you could let me release her hip as I have been trained to do and see if your daughter could walk better. She asked me to do what I need to do to help her daughter walk properly.

I laid the child on her stomach and positioned her leg in the right place, then with one maneuver, I heard this pop, and then I laid the child on her back and pulled on the leg. Her hip came free. I picked her up off the exam table and told her to walk. Her mom began to cry as she watched her child walk straight for the first time. I had a follow-up in a few months, and the child still walked straight. A year later, I had the child come back. She ran up to me, gave me a big hug, and that was the last time I saw that little girl. The amazing thing was that I did not need X-rays or an MRI; all I did was listen to the body and follow the principles that I learned.

You Bred the Mexican out of Him

By this time, we had moved out of the rental house from my in-laws. And we got into our new house. It was nice to have our own place and yard for the kids to play in.

The day before Levi was born, I was called into a deposition. One of the nursing homes was being sued by the patient who fell in the transport van. The patient was defending me and claimed Dr. Robison saved my life. The nursing home lawyers were saying otherwise. My thoughts were only on the birth of my child as I sat there being interrogated. I explained to the lawyers that there were doctor orders for antibiotics for his ulceration and infection, and I remember signing them. Their whole premise was that I never wrote the orders. When I caught them in their bluff, and they researched the missing order, it somehow appeared. After this stressful event, I was released from any wrongdoing. I went home to be with my wife, who was about to give birth.

The next day, as my wife's labor pains were increasing, her contractions were closer together, and we were still waiting for the water to break. While the midwife was mulling over whether to go to the hospital or not, my wife went into the bathroom, and I followed her. She found a comfortable position, and she started to push. The head was crowning, and then the water broke, and this child came out swimming, not a drop of blood on him; he was born in the fluid sac.

Levi was my sensitive child. He could pick up on others' emotions quickly. As he grew up, he always wanted to be right there with his older brother and sister at their sporting events. Because he was the only one of the children with blue eyes, his mom's side of the family would joke around by saying that we bred the Mexican out of him.

Levi loved asking me questions. One day, he asked me what hell was like. I responded, "You like to learn, don't you?" He said yes.

"Hell is a place that you cannot learn; you're stuck with what you know. It's like being stuck in the first grade when you should be in high school," I explained. "I don't want to go to hell; I want to learn as much as I can," he answered.

On another occasion with Levi, I was teaching him how to pray. I told him you can ask God anything, and if your faith is strong enough, God will deliver what you ask for. He asked, "Can I pray now?" I said you can pray anytime. He said, "I want it to snow tonight."

Living in Arizona, there is very little snow where we live, but I said, "OK, go ahead and say your prayer." He knelt by his bedside and started to pray. He was very specific in his prayers and asked God to allow it to snow tonight, and after closing his prayer, he jumped into bed. I, on the other hand, had to go and say a prayer myself. I had not seen it snow in a long time, but I always knew God would deliver. The next morning, Levi got up and ran to the window to look outside, and noticed the ground was covered in white. Now, I did not have any snow machine, nor did I go and spray white paint on the ground. There was actual snow on the ground. It may not have lasted long, but it snowed that night. I hope he will always remember this experience so he can rely on God.

While I was enjoying the three children, my wife and I prayed to see if we should have another child. There were times that I felt like I could see movements out of the corner of my eye; it was as if this child was darting across the room when there was no one there. I told my wife that we should have another child, and she agreed.

Using the Art of Jin Shin Jyutsu in Giving Birth

Early into my holistic training, I was learning this Japanese pressure point. Not fully knowledgeable in the study, I relied on calling my mentor the day Madalyn decided to be born. We knew she was a girl, as she was the only one of our children who had an ultrasound to see the sex of the baby. Her birth was the most difficult one of all of them. I really don't know the full reasons why it was more difficult. There was more stress, and the subtle, silent nights and the uncomfortable days when my wife's parents would come over, giving me small hints that something was brewing. She was also born at home, like all the others, but with more added stresses of life.

While the midwife was helping my wife, I was on the phone with my mentor. He was telling me about the places to hold my wife, who was in labor. The midwife said, "Whatever you're doing, keep doing it; the baby is coming." As I held the point to cause the dilation, I then repositioned my hands and held the points to allow the birth of the baby through the birth canal. She was a happy baby girl.

After all the excitement of the birth of Madalyn, I was back at work shortly after her birth. I also opened a clinic in the valley, which took more time away from the family.

I started to get involved with the schools by being on the school board and helping with coaching basketball. I also got involved in Scouting with my oldest boy.

We would have our family vacations and trips. On Easter, we would go back to my parents' house, where the kids could play with their cousins. We usually ended up building snow bunnies for Easter as it always snowed.

On the other hand, the 4th of July was a time when they could really play with their cousins. We would even go camping, and I would take the kids fishing and on our annual Mexico family vacation to Rocky Point.

Once again, my wife and I discussed another child. I had prayed about it and felt the impression to enjoy the four we had, and she agreed. If there was one thing that I tried to teach my children is to love each other. Friends will come and go, but your brothers and sisters will always be there.

Life could not be more complete. I had my private practice, and I helped bring our four children into the world. I was a husband, a father, a doctor, and involved in the community.

Reflection

In the arc from national tragedy to personal trials, from a struggling clinic to a calling reshaped by a daughter's healing, the throughline is simple: when life tests you, lead with faith, humility, and action. I learned that growth often hides inside discomfort, that health is built on daily choices, and that courage sometimes means changing course when the evidence of hope appears.

Miracles show up in quiet rooms and crowded vans, in a child's first prayer to God, only to show a snowy Arizona morning—but they meet us most readily when we listen, learn, and serve. Expertise matters, yet compassion, curiosity, and integrity matter more; they turn skills into healing and moments into meaning.

Approach every situation by being present, asking for help when needed, trusting what your body and conscience tell you, and doing the next right thing with gratitude. In the end, purpose isn't found at the finish line—it's forged along the way, in the love we give our families, the relief we bring our patients, and the faith that carries us forward one brave decision at a time.

CHAPTER 11

When You Hear the Birds Sing

*And so rock bottom became the solid
Foundation on which I rebuilt my life.*

– J.K. Rowling

Does Accomplishing Your Goals Have a Consequence?

Driven by goals my entire life, from getting into college to going on a medical mission to Tonga, to paying off my student loans by the age of 40, and the one main goal of having a family, I had accomplished them all. I wonder how many of us are indirectly affected by accomplishing our goals. We set our minds to what we want, we are determined to get it, and when we accomplish our desired goals, there is a paradigm shift.

When I paid off the student loan, I called my father and told him. As he was always concerned with my debt, he responded, "Don't get yourself back in debt," then concluded, "With that kind of money you spent on school, you could have been a real doctor." Hearing those words from my hero was gut ranching but I still respected him. I knew in my heart that I was a real doctor and did not have an MD or DO behind my name, but what mattered to me was how I saw myself as patients saw me.

Did my determination to learn as much of the holistic medicine approach have an effect on my family? Yes, both good and bad. The Good: I was able to help more patients holistically with positive results, but the consequence was that I was doing less surgery in my private practice, as I was doing more things naturally. I did not need to do as much surgery as I was trained to do. The bad effect was that there were frequent comments by my wife as to why I was not doing more surgery, as it was the main cash cow that brought most of the money in. The more I learned about Myopractics, the less money came in, even though my treatments were benefiting my patients.

Finding the Balance Between Professional Life and Family Life

Life is always looking for balance, whether it is the food we eat, as talked about in *Healthy Dad Sick Dad*, or in the workplace, with family and professional life, like I talk about in *Success DNA*. I did my best to take the family on vacations and trips, but I must be honest with you, I had a mother-in-law who had to be a part of every little thing in our marriage. Every time I took my family on a trip, she had to know where we were and was constantly on the phone while we were trying to enjoy our family vacation. On one trip, I purposely left the phones at home. This did not sit well with her. She was waiting at our house, demanding a reason for not checking in with her. I wish that were the only time, but it was not, and happened quite frequently.

Too Many Hands in the Health Care System

To add fuel to the fire, on November 20th, 2010, my private practice that I had for 10 years changed with a stroke of a pen. The new healthcare bill that was put into place took over 60 percent of my patients away from my practice. The state government felt my profession did not need podiatry services anymore, and here I was practicing in these rural communities where most of my patients had this state access plan. This was gone, and on top of that, I was asked to find a new location for both my clinic locations. Talk about being stressful. I had a choice to do more surgery to make up the difference in being paid or stay true to my inner conviction by providing a holistic approach to medicine. I chose to stay true to myself.

Get out, and You Have One Week to Do It

June of 2011: I finished paying off the house and we were finally debt-free. The student loans were paid off, the vehicles were paid off, and the house was paid off.

I took the kids to Utah for the 4th of July 2011 celebration. Levi, Jesa'Lyn, and Logan went with me; Madalyn stayed home with her mom. When we returned, I was told by my wife that her mother was so distressed when I took the kids to Utah that she bled in places she cannot mention. She went on to say, "When you get the divorce, make sure Glen cannot take the kids to Utah." I asked, "What are you talking about? What divorce?" She said, "I am only telling you what my mother said."

Logan had his 11th birthday when I was asked to speak in church. When I came home, my wife told me to get out. I have until Friday to get out. She wants a separation with possible divorce; there was no explanation, no reasons as to why. I was stunned; I was asked to get out, and I had five days to do it.

I really don't know if there was one thing or multiple things that caused this moment. Was it because I stood up to her mother, trying to run our family, or was it because we were finally debt-free, or maybe it was the financial crunch that happened to my medical practice with government cuts? I was doing fewer surgeries because of my success in helping patients get better in more of a natural way. I remember I asked my wife why she was doing this.

"Do you remember the day I asked if you wanted more children after Madalyn?" she asked. I said yes. "Well, I lied, I wanted more children, but not with you. I never loved you from the beginning. I wish you had stayed in Las Vegas. Why did you follow me back to Arizona? You need to get the hell out of here and go back home to Utah, where you belong."

I was speechless, and everything inside of me wanted to react.

Trying to juggle work and now finding a place to live, I packed what I could and loaded up my car, and found an apartment in the valley. Over the course of a few months, the children never knew anything about my reason for why I just moved. The nights were very quiet, and I did not sleep much. My mind would not stop working out; it was on a treadmill that would not stop. I was trying to do everything to save my marriage. But every idea came to a dead end. I persisted no matter what she had said to me.

The last time I ever talked to my mother-in-law, I happened to be at the house. I was in the kitchen as Levi came running through the front door. As he ran into the kitchen, where I was, his grandmother was right behind him, unaware that I was at the house. She screamed to Levi, "You little shit, get back here."

I stepped out and said, "Don't you ever talk to my child that way." I could see her head ready to explode and lash out at me, as I saw her true side. She left without an argument.

I remember on Thanksgiving, I went up to see the kids. We were only separated at the time, and the divorce papers were never served yet. My wife had prepared a Thanksgiving dinner that I was not allowed to attend. She was kind enough to leave me some food, and I slept out in the trailer that we had parked in the backyard.

The next morning, she arranged a family photo shoot for Christmas postcards. I thought that this may be a peace offering, and we were getting back together. She smiled through each photo taken. That next Monday, while I was in the clinic, a friend of mine walked into the clinic and saw me in the hallway as I was heading to see another patient. He asked me how I was. I said, "Great, how are you?" He suddenly pulled out an envelope and handed it to me, and said, "I am sorry I had to do this, but here are your court order papers."

I had just been served divorce papers right in the middle of the clinic, right after the photos were taken, just a little over a day ago. What kind of person would do that? I later learned that the photos were sent out to all her friends and family as if nothing had happened.

Still, trying to save my marriage even after the divorce papers were served, I once asked an older and wise man for advice on saving my marriage. He said, "Have you turned every stone over?" I said, "Yes, every stone is now gravel."

"Then there is nothing more you could do. Let it go and trust in God."

I continued to go to the required marriage counseling, but that was a complete joke. I think the marriage counselor was going through his own problems and did not give much counsel.

The following week, he asked each of us if the marriage was worth saving. I said, "Yes." My wife answered, "Not in a million chances." Surprisingly, this gave me hope; people win the lottery at those odds. I still tried to save the marriage.

Once I realized that the only reason she was still being nice to me was that she had this list that she wanted to complete before the divorce. Every item on the list required a cost. After doing four of them, I caught on to what she was doing when she wanted all the rooms in the house painted, when I had just paid for a new dishwasher and other things in the house. I now said no. She made one more request: "Could I please keep the house as it will not disrupt the kids in their schooling?" I gave in and agreed that I would give her the house that was completely paid off. It did not take her long to sell the house after the divorce, and she made double the amount of what I had paid for it.

The whole divorce proceeding went fast. Filed in December, the first court appearance happened in February, and then the divorce was finalized in May. It was official, but the court appearances did not end for the next seven years. I was in court twice a year, every year. It was around the time of the 4th of July, when I was used to taking my time off work to enjoy my favorite holiday, and the other time was during Christmas, usually the day after, so my time with the kids was always interrupted by this court date.

I was required to pay for both lawyers by the courts. She had hired a high-profile attorney in the financial district off Camelback Road in Phoenix. And I went through lawyers faster than crap coming out of an ex-laxed butthole. It was as if I were paying for the two lawyers who were both fighting against me. I remember one time, I had to pay for a professional psychologist who was an authority on parent alienation. She was asked in court by my lawyer, "When Glen goes and sees his daughter at school, and his daughter is hesitant to see him, the daughter says my mom does not want me to see my dad; is that parent alienation?"

"No," she replied, "that is just an indifference in parenting." After seven years of dealing with stuff like this, I found a lawyer who did not put up with crap and had an interest in my case and not the money that she could get out of it, being that I was a doctor.

A week after the divorce was finalized, I went to pick up my children to take them to see my parents. I made sure that my parents also got to enjoy their grandkids, contrary to what the other side wanted. I loaded the kids up in the truck and was going to a swim meet before heading out of town.

My ex was standing by the door wishing the kids goodbye, and one of them asked why Mom was not coming with us. I stopped what I was doing and asked my ex, "You never told the children that we are divorced?" It was the first time the kids had heard of anything of the sort. They learned that day we were divorced, almost a year later, from being kicked out of the house. They were told I ran off with a young woman, but that was not possible, because I never even went on a date for a year and a half after the separation and divorce. I was faithful to her. I never cheated on her or stepped out with another woman, and I went to work to provide for my family. I supported them as any father would do.

One day in the clinic, I talked with the chief of police. I was informed that it was a good thing that I was divorced. "By now, everyone knew about it in our small town." I was told it was a good thing because I do not know about the family I was once married to. Maybe I didn't want to know. I knew something was wrong the next day of my marriage, and now that was confirmed.

The Toll the Divorce Took on My Kids

I don't know what was said to the children, but one thing I quickly learned from a divorce is that the kids are the ones who suffer the most. Little by little, each one of my children said it was too much for them to be picked up on a Friday afternoon and go to the valley a good hour away, and then turn around and wake up at 4:00 a.m. on a Monday to get ready to go back to their hometown and go to school. As they got older, their activities required them to stay home on my days that I was assigned to them. It first started with Logan, the oldest. I think he had the hardest time knowing his parents were no longer together. This child, I would take with me everywhere when he was young. I would be there for all his baseball and soccer practices, and I even participated in some of the scout camps that he was involved in. As for my oldest daughter, she also decided to stay home on her days when the courts order her to be with me. This was my little girl who changed the course of my medical career. There was no more running into my arms or the bright brown eyes staring up at her dad.

I remember one day in the early stages of the divorce, I went to go and pick up the kids. Jesa'Lyn had made chocolate chip cookies. "Dad, I made you cookies. Try one." She handed me one while her mom was standing there in the kitchen. I had not eaten any chocolate in over 20 years, but I took her cookie and gladly ate it. Her mom commented, "Well, that is something I have never seen." I just smiled and enjoyed the cookie because I knew it was made with love.

My youngest daughter was next to stay home. She just said she was too tired and did not feel well. She was so young that I don't know how much she knew of me. I have many photos of her with us fishing and traveling. She was truly the last one who came up to me and gave me a big hug and said, "I love you, Dad." I know there were times when I would go up to the elementary school and ask to see her. They would page for her, and she would walk through the main office doors. She would look around very hesitantly; I guess to see if her mom was around. As she sat there on the bench, in front of all the secretaries, there would be no questioning as to my being with my daughter. I would just talk with her. She said to me, "Mom does not want me to see you." I said, I know. It was not long after this that she, too, stopped coming in my days.

My youngest son Levi was the last to go; he stayed with me a good year after the other ones chose to stay back with their mother. He told me it was hard for him to come because when he got home, he would be drilled by his other brother and sisters and his mother as to why he went to see his father. Levi was very sensitive and did not like any arguments. He asked me if it was OK to stay back home. I remembered the last time I spoke with him; I asked him what he wanted to do, and he said I really want to keep coming and see you, but I feel I need to stay home. We both shed some tears that morning, and I took him back home. He said I will see you when I am eighteen. He is now 19 years old, and only the memories of my last visit with him remain in my thoughts and heart. I still have hope that one day he will knock on my door.

It took me seven years to find a good lawyer who had my back and would fight for me in court. I only showed up once more in court after hiring her; it was the shortest hearing that I had in the courts. After the hearing, she said to me that she has seen cases like this in her practice, and it does not sit well with the parent who keeps fighting for the children. Something usually happens that is not good, like one parent usually ends up in jail for a false allegation or something even more horrific. She went on to say, "If it were me, I would step away and just let time heal things."

It was the hardest thing I had to do in my life, letting go of the fight inside to see my children persistently. This was my choice. I always send them a card for their birthday and Christmas, and even texted and called them a few times, but never got a response. No responses on Father's Day or my birthday. It was as if I were dead to them, even though they cashed their checks that were sent in the cards. I had no idea the toll this was going to take on me. All I know is my love for my children was beyond anyone's comprehension. They were everything to me.

Rock Bottom Hurts When You Hit It

I reflected on the many times when the kids were young, they would always look up in the sky at night and say, "Dad, the moon is broken, can you fix it?" I would look up in the night sky and see the moon was showing a quarter percent or God's thumbnail. I said to them, "Yes, I will fix it, but give me a few days." A few days later, when the moon was full, they would look up in the dark sky of the night and say, "Dad, you fixed the moon." I just smiled. I would miss these moments, saying things like they would call ketchup "dip up" because you were always dipping your fries in it.

One of the hardest things to hear was when people would say, "Oh, you will see your kids again." I would say no. When I do see them, they will no longer be kids; they will be adults if they choose to come and see me. It was as if these kids of mine were kidnapped, and all I have are the memories to go by. I will never be able to get this back. Still, I also understand that living in bitterness and anger damages not only our mind but our physical body, so all I can do is remember the good times and forgive the hard times.

To conclude with the kids, even though I do not see them, I have not given up on hope that maybe one day they will knock on my door.

But with that said, I am not going to wait around for them to show up. I need to live my life and serve and help people. I will never stop praying for them every day, and I will welcome them with open arms should they choose to come back.

Outing with my four children in the white mountains.

Life was different. The nights were dead silent. The meals had one set of plates when I sat down to eat. The people at church treated me like I had AIDS; they did not want to talk with a divorced person. And if they did, they wanted to know what I did to cause the divorce. I was literally a prisoner in my own environment. I spent so many sleepless nights alone in my apartment and would not even venture out and meet people. My emotions took a toll on me.

On the one night I fell asleep, I was immediately woken with this pain in my foot that would not go away. I drove myself to my clinic to give myself a shot to ease the pain. I tried to recall the time I cut off the tip of my finger with a bread knife, and all my wife when

I was still married could do was laugh at me while I bandaged up my finger and drove myself to the hospital. Even though this experience did not cause me to be angry, I was still in so much anguish, missing my children.

I never got to the point where I wanted to take my life. I have heard of people who have, but I don't know what the last thought was that caused them to end their physical life. Still, I am sure there was a sense of pure frustration, and so deep was the despair that there was no hope for any word or event to change things. My heart aches for them and their loved ones who they left behind. Frustration is different than depression. Frustration requires you to step out of the environment that is causing you to be frustrated. Once you step out, the world looks different, and you can move on, but it is a choice. Whereas depression is much more seeded hurt, but you cannot dance and be depressed at the same time, that is something they don't tell you. All the medical profession will do is give you a pill to swallow.

At some point in life, we will have to face our Abrahamic moment. It will push you to the brink of saying this is too much for me to handle, but there is a promise in the scriptures that God will not give you more than what you can handle. I felt I was pushed beyond my point of handle, but maybe God saw something that I could not see in myself. He saw my true potential and was refining me to the point that I could see it also. Out of the greatest tragedy of life comes the greatest blessing, and those hidden talents come to the present. The key is you must participate in the process, so look at these events as a teaching opportunity, a mental exercise that your mind must go through just like your body does at the gym, and you will see your true potential. I keep telling myself that the harder and more difficult the situation I go through, the greater the blessing will be. Don't be afraid of it, but instead welcome it.

The day I packed my bags and went to a place to be alone by myself, I sat in the garage and just wanted to close my eyes and see the bright lights again, like I once experienced. After having a lengthy conversation with myself, I opened the garage. I drove myself back to my place in the valley. Maybe God had something for me to do, and maybe he was about to show me a few hidden talents.

Shortly after this event, I was having a conversation with a friend, and he asked, "Have you heard the birds sing?" I was puzzled. "Have you heard the birds chirp?" he asked again.

It made me stop and think; had I even heard one bird chirp or sing since my divorce? I realize that, indeed, I had not heard one in years. I was so wrapped up in my head about the loss of my children that I lost focus on the blessing that was in front of me.

The day I heard my first bird chirp was the day I started to truly give thanks and appreciation for what I had in front of me. Gratitude is a key element to healing your soul. When my knees hit the floor every morning and night, I give thanks for all the blessings in my life, and for the birds that chirp and sing.

Reflection

When life hits its deepest lows, it also lights the brightest fires of growth. This chapter shows that staying anchored to your core values and choosing integrity over ease can transform even the hardest trials into tomorrow's triumphs. Your path may weave through conflict, loss, and doubt, but these moments are fuel for resilience, clarity, and purpose. Practical wisdom emerges, cultivating daily gratitude, listening for the subtle signs of possibility amid chaos, and turning setbacks into deliberate steps forward.

Embrace courageous choices, nurture your well-being, and communicate with honesty and compassion—even when it's tough. Move forward with a bold, hopeful heart, knowing that every challenge is an invitation to learn, expand your capabilities, and build a future shaped by courage, kindness, and relentless perseverance.

CHAPTER 12

If You Could Ask God a Question

Your heartbeat plays my favorite song.

– Xanthi

What if you could ask God a question and have a direct answer immediately, like two people talking in a coffee shop? What would you ask? Here are some questions I asked God right after my divorce. 1. Where do I live? 2. What do I do about being on the school board? 3. What about my finances? 4th, a question I could not verbalize, but just thought it. All the questions had an immediate answer, but the last one really surprised me when I got the answer.

God Knew My Thoughts When I Could Not Speak Them

If there is one thing that I dislike hearing after my divorce, it is the question "How are you doing?" And the quote that time heals everything. How can time heal when God does not wear a watch?

I followed the answers that I got when I talked to God. I moved to Gilbert in the valley, resigned from the school board, and kept the assurance that I would make it financially. To the fourth question that I could not verbalize–would I remarry? –The answer came to me as walking in on a surprise birthday party.

You're speechless at first, then you have to chuckle. God said, "Yes, I have someone prepared for you." I immediately believed that God was going to match me up with someone. I wonder who he will send my way as the days turned into weeks and the weeks into months and the months into years. I went back to the same place after about a year and a half of being on my own to ask God again when he would be sending me that person. I just got the impression soon.

I dove deep into the art of Jin Shin Jyutsu and Myopractics, and I learned more levels of the technique. It required me to be in person. This was good for me, as I had to interact with other people. I also joined the gym and got my own personal trainer to help me work out physically and put my built-up tension of frustrations, anger and sorrow, and despair into the weights. I continued to eat healthy and not gravitate to the foods that could give me the quick but short sugar highs.

How I Have Taken My Emotions and Helped My Diabetic Patients

I remember one day, I was introduced to an agent who was marketing a common diabetic device. Back then, it was still in trial and was only used on type I diabetics. It was a device to show you your blood sugar without having to stick your finger. All you had to do was place the device with a little fine wire underneath the skin on your stomach area, and place a cover on top of it for protection from water, and you wear it. I asked if I could try out this device, as I was trying to see what foods helped diabetics and what foods harmed diabetics.

What I learned from this device was everything I mentioned in my book, *Healthy Dad Sick Dad*: ginger, blueberries, green beans, and cinnamon lower blood sugar. What I also learned was that bread and pizza, and other high-carb foods would also spike the blood sugars. I was very impressed by how ginger lowered the blood sugar and fast. But I was also amazed that while lying in bed and thinking of the past events with the children and the divorce, my sugar just spiked, with no food involved. I also noticed the blood reading would go down when I changed my thoughts to loving myself and feeling the love of those around me. I guess what I am trying to say here is that emotion, along with food, influences your body and your health, and yes, your emotions are at the forefront of all diseases, along with unful-filled inner desires.

With this new knowledge, emotions, and how they aided in the development of diabetes. I knew I had to make changes. I heard of a man who practiced up in St George, Utah, who could help with spiritual healing. I only had one session with him, but he said something to me. He said you need to forgive your past and your parents. Something happened when your mother was in her third trimester.

I left his clinic and drove up to see my parents. The 3-hour drive gave me time to forgive many people. I did not turn on the radio; I just forgave every single person that came up in my mind, from the high school counselor to the coach in high school. I even forgave my ex and mother-in-law for all the crazy things she did (She was the one that I had to forgive 70 times 7, like the bible said to do). I forgave my former wife and everyone associated with her.

When I arrived home, I asked my parents what had happened in the last trimester before I was born. I learned that my father was out of work, and my mother had breast cancer, but it had not been detected yet. They both wondered how they were going to feed another child. I would be number seven, and they had already lost one before me. All their emotions went right to me, and I did not even know about it. I was just unaware of it. I forgave them and drove back home to Arizona. I can say I have truly forgiven my past. Because I did not want diabetes because of sorrow and grief, nor did I want heart problems because of anger and frustration.

Will I Ever Remarry? Are You from Canada?

Going back to the fourth question, yes, I was going to remarry, and yes, God is going to be my matchmaker! I wonder what kind of woman he would be sending me. I asked myself. I know he has a sense of humor, as I have seen this multiple times in my life. It took me a while after the divorce to even go on a date. I would be lined up and would decline; I did not want to go back into this dating life again, as I experienced in high school, college, and even medical school.

After being divorced for a year, my church leader encouraged me to get out there and date. I tried a few times, but it was not for me. The whole trying to impress was not my thing, and I was rusty with approaching someone and asking them to go out. I approached God again and said to him, "You told me you had someone prepared for me. I have been on a few dates, but I just am not comfortable with the dating scene."

I again got the impression as if someone was talking to me. Don't worry, it will be soon. Now, in God's time, one day is a thousand years; I don't think I could wait a thousand years. Even though I was patient with the answer, my mind was not patient and was questioning, would it be tomorrow, or a month, or maybe years from now.

I always know you must do your part when you offer a prayer to the heavens. So many of us sit around and wait for the answer to happen. I feel you must participate in the process. It is like a joint adventure. When you pray for wealth, do you sit around waiting for the money tree to drop hundred-dollar bills? No, you must put in some sweat and effort and participate. Well, I had just done that, and went on two dates, I showed I was putting myself out there. But after two dates, I was done. I was not giving up, but I did explain to God that I was so out of touch with the dating life that it was uncomfortable to me beyond my stress levels. If he wanted me to marry again, he would have to send me someone.

Shortly after this conversation with God, my brother had told me that I should read a book about a man who died four times and wrote about each event. This was the same brother whom I promised that I would go to his wedding when I had my near-death experience. I got the book, and I read it. Then I reported back to him. I said the first death that the man experienced is what I experienced. Still, I was more curious about the death he had when he was on an island in the Pacific Ocean. He described being visited by a woman this time. She was tall, with olive skin and long jet-black hair. She said she was from northern Canada. Then she left him, and he came back from his near-death experience. I then jokingly told my brother that if God wants me married, then he will send me someone just like that woman I read about. The book was a good read.

A week prior to reading the recommended book, I was in my out-of-town clinic. I was going about my day when this man, whom I knew, came in and caught me in the hallway. Only he was not serving me papers, but a message. He said, "I felt impressed that I need to tell you this: Second marriages are better than the first." I am sure he did not give that counsel out to everyone. Still, he spoke those words as if they were a personal message from heaven. This was the start of things to come.

Three days from the time I joked about that woman in the book to my brother, I was in my clinic in the valley. I had just come out of the treatment room when my staff was taking someone back to a treatment room. She realized all the rooms were filled, so she started to take the patient back to the waiting room. I made eye contact with the patient, and time just froze.

This woman had jet black hair, olive skin, and was tall; it was as if she stepped out of the book. I asked for the chart, looked down, and caught her age. I chuckled inside and realized God's humor. I saw her age; she was a lot younger than me, but God knew she was old enough to date. This is where it all began. I told my staff to have her take a seat in my office, and I would be right there.

I finished up with the patient that I was working on and went into my office and introduced myself to her. She said her name was Xanthi. She was so impressed with the painting on the walls that she asked about the artist.

"I did them over twenty years ago. These are painting I did in college," I said to her humbly. "Are you ready for me to look at what is going on with your feet?" I then asked. She nodded her head. I took her down the hallway and into the exam room. I figured out what was going on with her foot and told her to come back in two weeks. She was a ballet dancer, but was side-lined with this foot injury.

Xanthi with a surprise lunch visit at work.

I maintained my professional manner and treated her. Still, my mind took its own adventures of wondering, was this the person God sent me? It was everything that I envisioned when I read that book. So many things raced through my mind; I wondered about what I had read and visualized, to actually seeing this person in real life, and was it really what God had prepared for me? I immediately stopped these thoughts; she is my patient, and I can't date a patient, and even if I could, she is too young for me.

Two weeks went by, and she came back into the office. Xanthi was on my schedule to be seen when she was placed in the exam room. I asked her how her foot was doing. She said it is much better. "So, are you going back to dance?" I asked. She said no, not at this time, and then she asked, "Would you like to go out sometime?"

Feeling embarrassed, she held back, "Oh, I am so sorry; I did not ask if you are married. Are you?"

"No, I am not married, and yes, I would like to go out with you." Curious, I asked her if she happened to be from Canada? She laughed and said, "No, why?" I said, "Oh, nothing."

We went out, and things just clicked. I really enjoyed being with her, although I struggled so much with her age. But when I was with her, I did not see her age; it was only the time that I was not with her that my mind created doubts.

We went on our first date to an organic restaurant; she was into health and beauty. I explained that if we dated, she could not be my patient, and she said that was quite all right with me. We saw each other on and off for several months. She did not have a phone, so we corresponded by email. I waited at least four months to introduce her to my kids. She was so good to them. Their mother, on the other hand, felt threatened by her, even though she had already started a relationship right after the divorce and had her boyfriend move in just after the divorce was finalized.

A few months into dating and corresponding by email, I again struggled with the thought of being too old for her. I recall one day I was in my office, and my front staff employee came to me and reported that there was a gentleman who wanted to see me. I said, "Bring him in." He was a former patient of mine; I had not seen him in years.

He said, "I was at Costco, and I got this strong impression to stop by your office on my way back home, and here I am. I feel I need to tell you something, and I don't know why I am telling you this, but here it goes. I had the best time with my wife over the years until she passed away. I was bothered by her age difference when I first married her, but when I married her, her age did not matter to me. There was a 20-year age difference between us."

Then he said that was what I needed to tell you and walked out of the office. I have never seen that man again. I sat and pondered what he had said, and with him not knowing I was dating and seeing someone younger than me, and no prior knowledge of me dating a young woman, let alone being divorced. That day, my thoughts changed. I have never had an issue with her age again. Did God send me another message from heaven? I believe he did.

What you want wants you! I learned Xanthi wanted the same thing I wanted. She told me that when she was young, at the age of 4, she had seen in her mind a set of blue eyes on a man that she would be with one day. That day she walked into my office, she saw those same blue eyes, and knew there was something special about me.

My First Book I Ever Wrote

When I proposed to her, I did not do the Christmas lights as before, but I wrote my first book. I found a leather-bound book with blank pages in it. On the front cover was sketched a tree of life. I just added some words on the cover that said: *Xanthi, My Angel. I just feel safe when I am around you.* I took quotes that she would have me read and placed them on the blank pages. I also enclosed photos of us that went along with those quotes. This entailed the first half of the book. In the last half of the book, I glued the papers together, then I cut a hole in the middle of those glued pages and placed the ring that was wrapped in satin cloth. Then I placed a photo of a couple in a rice field over the hole that I had cut out. It was like a secret compartment in the book.

On the previous page, I wrote: "If I could take you to the rice fields, I would. I hope that the cabin will be sufficient, so let me take the rice field to you. Look closely, you will find my love of my life deeper in the field. I will always love you, Your Glen."

I had cut out the photo right over the cut-out glued papers, and as she saw one of the edges lifted. She lifted open the photo, and on the back of it said, "Great, you found it. Will You…" Then she took out the satin cloth and found the ring. And then I finished the sentence by saying "Marry Me?"

And of course, she said yes.

The day we got married, 8/8/2013 at 8:08 p.m., made me smile even bigger. I said a little prayer to God and thanked him for sending her to me. He then said, as he had previously done in a clear voice: "Be good to her; she is one of my precious daughters."

You could say that all the time that God spoke to me was only my thoughts. I could agree with you to a point, but the only thing that makes me stand by my conviction is how it was said. Those words were not my words but were said with strong emotion and feelings. I know when I have conversations with myself, when I am working out a solution to a problem or situation. I know my words; these were different.

She has been my rock; she helped me to see things I could not see and hear things that I could not hear, and feel things that I have never felt before. She has taught me that it is possible to love again. She bought me an easel with the hope that I would pick up painting again. It was her goal to see that I painted again. I say painting saved my life, it did, but it was really Xanthi that saved my life. She helped me see one of the God given talents that I could not see in myself, but she saw it. She patiently waited for years for me to pick up the brush to start painting again. Every day that I get to see her smile, listen to her voice, and feel her arms as they wrap around my chest to give me a hug is priceless. She will always be my earthly angel. Thank you, God, for sending her into my life at the right time.

Transforming My Profession One Brush Stroke at a Time

One of the most humbling experiences that I have ever experienced in life is taking a scalpel and opening the skin, going layer-by-layer, fixing what needed to be fixed, and then closing the skin the best way, trying to leave what was so pristinely put together before I made the cut. I was recently asked if it was hard to go from a scalpel to a paintbrush.

"Not really," I replied, "Now I am a plastic surgeon just without the blood. You want your nose fixed, I can do that; you want a tummy tuck, I can do that too; you want your eyes a different color, I can do that, and you will look as real as looking in a mirror."

Painting Saved My Life from the Darkest Days to the Brightest Nights

You would think I could end my book here, but what I have learned in life is, life never stops until the last breath we take. My frustration with the divorce and not being able to see the kids got to a tipping point, and I did question if it was worth remaining here. I said I was never depressed, as I still had hope and tried to find ways out of a situation that I did not like to be in, but this time, I could not see the way out. When children stop responding to me, no phone calls, no text messages, Reality sets in, knowing that I could never have a normal and loving conversation with them again. I felt cheated out of life. I was still called into court to see how much more money they could get out of me with child support. I feel this was her motive for having the kids with her full-time, as it made a different in how much I paid her for child support. If I saw the kids for one night, it would change the child support calculations. So, by keeping them from me, I had to pay the fullness of what I was ordered.

I had been blessed with a very loving and caring wife, a person who was more than just a wife; she was my best friend and my protector, but I let my inner mind develop a story that the pain became more than I could handle when I thought about my children. I had said my goodbye to my beautiful wife, thinking I would never see her again, drove myself to a far-off place, and sat there in the garage wanting to end my life. I am asked what caused me to stop what I was about to do. I knew that if I took my own life, once I did it would not have the bright lights and the peaceful feelings like the time I did when I was observing the medical team working on me. I would, in actuality, be stuck in the same frustration that took me to this place that caused me not to want to be here.

Then something happened, and I had one of those conversations again with myself, asking, "Do you really want to do this? You know if you take your own life, you're not going to the beautiful place you once experienced in medical school. You will remain frustrated. If you walk away, maybe God will show you how to paint again and use the easel your wife bought you, or there may be something else you will do that is not even on your radar."

Heavily in my mind, I chose to put all the negative thoughts aside and endure what was thrown at me. I started up the truck and pulled out of the garage, and made a call to my wife and told her I was heading home. I also said a silent prayer to God and asked him a favor. "Now that I am still here, could you please send someone to help me with the colors of the oils so I could start painting again?"

A few days later, I was in the clinic with a patient who broke her foot. I soon learned that she had studied realism art her entire life, and she learned what the masters learned. Over the course of months treating her, I never knew she painted. Her sister happened to come to the clinic with her on her last day, when I was to release her from the clinic. Somehow, we got on the topic of oil painting. I think something was said about one of my paintings in the room. The sister piped in: "My sister paints." I said, "You do?" She said in a humble way, "Yes, I do."

"Can you show me some of your paintings?" I requested. She pulled out her phone and showed me some of her paintings. It was all portraits, something I knew nothing about. But I noticed her colors were incredible, unlike anything I have ever seen before.

I asked her, "Do you give lessons?" She said no. I wanted to learn how to use colors, and I am struggling to get back into it, so I asked again, "Would you reconsider and just teach me one lesson on color?"

She told me she just sensed something about me and felt she needed to help me with this once. She had turned down so many others who had asked her. When she said she would give you one lesson, something subtlety shifted in my whole being.

A week later, I went to her art studio. She sat down with me, handed me a small 8x10 flat canvas along with a photocopy of a paper with multiple shades and shapes on it, and said, "Go home and paint what you see, and then bring it back, and I will decide if I will teach you my way of painting." I did just that and brought it back to her. She then broke out another canvas and said, "So you want to learn colors? I want you to paint this. It was a photo of three apples in a bowl." I painted it just like the shape assignment, but now with color. I must admit the apples looked like tomatoes.

"Can you teach me more?"

She replied with a question, "What is your purpose and goal in painting?" I said I would really love to paint my children the way I remember them. She told me that most people who paint want to get it done as soon as possible and put it on the wall or try to sell it. If this is your purpose and intention, then I cannot help you, but if you want to learn how to paint, I will help you.

I have now accomplished my goal of painting each child, and now, over seven years, I have over seventy paintings with a large variety of subjects. I have not sold one, and most of them are displayed in my clinic. Seeing them in person is much better than on a website, but if you're curious about my paintings, you can see all my artwork at www.drglenrobison.com.

Why I Use Painting in My Office

In most of my paintings, there are all the colors of the color wheel. I have learned that colors heal. Audrea Moritz talks about it in his healing books. Each color has a healing component;

the person viewing it has no idea, but it does heal the chakras of the body. When you walk into my waiting room, all you see are paintings; no magazines, no TV, just paintings. I know that if I can calm down a patient's mind before they are taken back to the treatment room, it makes my life much easier to work on them.

In my Office: The Painting of Christ and the American Flag

When I started to paint, I wanted to paint my children. When I accomplished that, I wanted to paint a Christ painting to hang on my wall in my house. There was a painting of Christ in my old church. When they decided to build a new building, everything in the building went up for auction. I wanted my dad to bid on that painting. I was so drawn to that painting, but being very young, I did not have the funds to put in a bid. It ended up being sold to my aunt, who has it in her house. I am thankful it is there. Little did I know it was one of those little seeds that was planted into my soul. At the time, I had an idea I could paint, and when I started to paint, I had no idea that I could do portrait painting. It probably took me a good 45 years later from that childhood experience that I painted my first Christ painting.

I did not have to put a bid in or buy one for my wall, I just painted Christ and personalized the painting with the American flag in the background. This same Christ painting, I had a copy in one of my treatment rooms. A patient who was very hesitant to see a doctor for his pain told me this when I was in the exam room with him. He said I am not an outgoing religious person, but I do a lot of silent prayers in my heart. I asked God to help me get out of pain, and so I looked for a podiatrist in the area. Your name came up, and I was anxious in your waiting room, as I don't like being in doctors' offices. Still, when your staff took me into this room, I noticed your painting of Christ and the American Flag, and I knew I was in the right spot. I told him thank you for sharing this with me and fixed his complaint, and have not seen him since.

When I moved into my new place two years ago, I made sure that this Christ and the American flag were the centerpiece in my waiting room. A minister told me in a church that I was brave to put Christ up in the waiting room. He asked, "What if someone comes into the office who is not a believer?"

I said, "The painting of Christ is for all, even if you're not a believer or of a different religion that only sees Christ as a prophet. I will still treat them the same and put my full focus on helping them get better."

What I have learned from painting can be summed up in three P's: Patient, Practice, and Perseverance. Be patient with yourself; Practice, Practice, and Practice (perfect practice makes perfect); and your perseverance will be rewarded, so be happy when you paint because each layer of paint will capture each emotion that you are feeling.

God and Country 18x24 oil on canvas painting.

Another Hidden Talent Discovered

In the fall of 2019, I approached one of my life's greatest weaknesses—the ability to write. My mind was always creative in putting the thoughts in my head of what I wanted to say. Still, each time I started to write, my words were not proper English, and it confused the teacher reading my assignment. The book *Health Dad Sick Dad: What good is your Wealth if you don't have your Health?* became a bestseller in aging, alternative medicine, and diabetes when it was released in June of 2020.

Most books, if they don't sell right at the beginning, usually do not sell. This book is like that silent snowball on top of the hill, just slowly making its way down the mountainside. One day, it will have so much force that a little snowball will be an avalanche and flood the earth with its information that will better the health of everyone. It is hard to believe that I wrote a bestseller book for someone who could not even spell chocolate in the 6-grade spelling bee.

Xanthi 16x20 oil on canvas painting.

It is my own personal feeling that out of a tragedy comes some of your greatest blessings. Xanthi has shown me a love that I had never experienced in a very long time. I think the closest thing to it was when I was with my mom in the garden. I felt safe, I felt like I learned more, and I felt an unconditional love. Maybe one day she will write her own book on her wisdom and knowledge that resides in her old soul and express them through her youthful vigor.

Reflection

Your story is a roadmap: Ask boldly, listen quietly, and then move your feet–because guidance meets you in motion. Choose forgiveness to free your heart, guard your mind because thoughts shape your health, and nourish your body like it carries your mission–because it does. Do your part and trust God's timing; keep your integrity and watch better doors appear. Turn pain into purpose–create, serve, and let beauty rebuild you one brave brushstroke at a time. When fear whispers, answer with the three P's: Patience to let the process work, Practice to sharpen your gifts, and Perseverance to finish what you started.

Put reminders of faith where you can see them, surround yourself with color that calms, and keep people who lift you close. If darkness presses in, choose life, and ask for help. When a sign appears, say yes. When doubt rises, breathe, bless the moment, and take the next right step. Live as a partner with God–consistent in effort, open to miracles–and meet every new situation with courage, clarity, and compassion.

That's how hope becomes health, and how your life becomes a testimony that better is not just possible–it's promised to the willing.

CHAPTER 13

If Feet Could Speak, What Would They Say?

"God gives the mango;
The farmer plants the seed,
God cures the patient;
The doctor takes the fees."

— Hindu Proverb

Real Life Experiences with Patients Throughout the Years

Save a toe, save a foot, save a limb, save a life: that has been my motto since starting my own private practice. I have silently been transforming my profession day by day. Here are a few of those feet as they tell their stories while I worked on them in the clinic.

How I Incorporated Jin Shin Jyutsu into My Practice

Jin Shin Jyutsu is an ancient Japanese art of harmonizing the body's life energy through gentle, light touch to restore balance and facilitate healing[2].

One day, I had an office staff member who was due to give birth to her child. She was told that if she were not at this level of contractions by the first of next week, she would be induced. She did not

____

[2] Jin Shin Jyutsu. (n.d.). *Jin Shin Jyutsu: An ancient art that promotes healing.* Retrieved October 22, 2025, from https://ukhealthcare.uky.edu/wellness-community/blog/jin-shin-jyutsur-ancient-art-promotes-healing

want to be induced, so she approached me the Friday afternoon, before the office was closed for the weekend. She told me what was going to happen; she then asked me if I could help her. After the clinic was done, I took her into a room and started to work on the points that I was taught to help deliver my last child. I held the points and did the flow, as they call it. I said, "OK, let me know if anything happens." I was anticipating a call on Monday saying she was going to be induced. That next morning, I got a call early, and it was her. She said, "I cannot thank you enough, but I gave birth last night."

I have worked on patients with Bell's palsy, "drooping of one side of the face," and seeing the correction come back. I mainly use this technique for relaxing the muscles in the legs when I need to release a certain joint. I also use it to help take the nausea completely out when someone who may have had surgery in the office and now wants to vomit. It is amazing that within 30 seconds, by holding certain points, you can take the nausea completely out.

I have found this technique very valuable, and it sets me apart from my colleagues when working with patients in the clinic.

How I Incorporate Myopractics into My Practice

Myopractics is a form of manual therapy and bodywork that focuses on releasing soft tissue restrictions to restore movement and balance in the musculoskeletal system[3].

Myopractics was introduced to me when my daughter had her life-changing experience. I started to learn this form of healing, it was like putting the body together like a puzzle, one piece at a time. Over the years, I have used it extensively and have taken patients out of pain before I would offer surgery or other means.

---

[3] Merrill Myopractics. (n.d.). *What is Myopractics?* Retrieved October 22, 2025, from https://www.mmyopractics.com/what-is-myopractics

I will share with you many experiences with this later in the chapter. What I can say is I studied extensively with my Healthy Dad (Mentor) and would travel to see him and spend weeks working with him while he worked on me. I got to work on him. On occasion, I got to see him in action when he had a client come in to be worked on. I observed how he communicated with the patient and how his hands went to work. What I found amazing was how Myopractics and Jin Shin Jyutsu complemented each other and would be used together in a treatment setting.

My studies in alternative medicine opened pathways that I didn't know existed. Just like me, who had herniated discs in the lower and upper back, I did not require a single shot or surgery to correct the condition. Yes, it took years of work, but it was well worth it.

I remember my brother calling me up one day and telling me he was just diagnosed with a herniated disk in his lower back, and asked me if I could work on him. He flew down and spent a few days with me over the weekend. Taking him through the three-step process, manipulation, releasing the compressed disks, and then integration of the energy back into the body with Jin Shin Jyutsu was a game-changer for him. He is back to hiking and golfing, and all the exercises he loved to do. When his doctor asked him about his back and if he had surgery, he responded, "No, I went to Arizona and was fixed without surgery."

On a follow-up visit a year later, he told me about his neck pain. I said it is your elbow and thumb, released both, and his pain went away.

Ankle Manipulation with Myopractics

Another man came into my office. He was having severe, unexplained pain in his ankles; he injured them on the job, but was not able to go back to work due to the pain. He, too, had been seeing doctor after doctor, and nothing was working. He had an MRI, but that was negative for any findings. All he wanted to do was go back to work. After examining him and finding the pressure point in the leg that told me his ankle was not tracking right, I told the patient what I was going to do by giving a tug on each ankle. There may be a popping sound, but it will not hurt, I assured him. I lay him completely back and got him to relax. Then, with the correct timing of his breaths, I executed the manipulation on the right ankle with a loud pop, then another loud pop on his left ankle. I held the area released to take the shock out of the tissue and then put his socks and shoes on (yes, a doctor who puts socks and shoes back on the patients). When he stood up, he stopped immediately and turned back to me and said, "What did you do? I have no pain in my ankles." I followed up with him a few weeks later, and he was still pain-free. I told him to follow up with me if anything should go south again. He went back to work, and I have not seen him in my clinic in over 17 years.

In my experience with this type of condition, it is very common for the joint to shift subtly; an MRI does not even pick it up. Hence, most patients go from doctor to doctor and spend enormous amounts of money and time on these outrageous pieces of plastic called inserts and various shoe specialty stores. Most of the time, they don't even need inserts in their shoes. Some will require a Prolotherapy shot, as I will describe in my next experience. But some need the release and good shoes, and they go on with life like nothing happened. I see this every week in my practice: Ankle sprains, old and new, at some point, in my opinion, will need this type of work done to be pain-free and have the movement back in the joint. If they don't, other things arise, like arthritis and tendonitis, and upper knee pains, and even hip pain.

I feel Western medicine goes directly to the point of pain or condition. In contrast, alternative or Eastern medicine goes to the source of the pain or condition that may be completely away from the expressed painful area.

First Prolotherapy Patient

Prolotherapy is a non-surgical, injection-based treatment used to strengthen and repair injured or weakened ligaments, tendons, and other connective tissues[4].

After getting my own experience with Prolotherapy by Dr Pomeroy, a world-renowned Prolotherapist who saw me twice, I had injured my right ankle on and off throughout high school, college, and every time I played basketball. I had a very unstable ankle. After the first treatment, I was impressed and followed up with him for the second time. I asked if he could train me in this specialty. He welcomed me back to the office to observe him with other patients.

As I shadowed him in the clinic, I saw his impressive skills. As I was walking down the hallway in his clinic, he had many photos of famous people with their notes of thanks to him. He defiantly helped thousands of patients over the years. I was fortunate to be trained by him, as a few years later he passed away, leaving a legacy filled with many of those he trained throughout his years in the clinic.

Shortly after my own personal experience, I wanted to try it out on someone. I had a patient lined up for surgery for tendon repair and an ankle stabilization procedure due to the weakness and pain in her ankle. I told her on the phone what I wanted to do. She canceled the surgery with her surgeon, which was only a few days out, and came in to have the Prolotherapy done on her injured ankle.

---

[4] Cleveland Clinic. (2022, February 28). *Prolotherapy: What it is, uses & side effects*. Cleveland Clinic. Retrieved October 22, 2025, from https://my.clevelandclinic. org/health/treatments/22426-prolotherapy

When she got to my clinic, I followed the protocol that was shown to me, but I released the ankle differently and then gave the shot. I instructed her on what to expect over the next month and had her come back in four weeks. When she came back, she was pain-free and out of the brace. I have followed up with her now for over 13 years, and her ankle is still as good as it was the day she followed up in my clinic after getting the Prolotherapy shot.

Professional Basketball Player: Manipulation with Prolotherapy

I went to the airport early one morning to catch my flight to work with my mentor. I always like to get to the airport two hours early, don't ask me why. As I was sitting there just reading one of my books, a man came by and sat right by me. He was friendly and started up a conversation. He told me he was flying back east to see his family. Still, he is kind of in limbo, as he was playing professional basketball in Europe and injured his ankle severely six months ago. He said they can't figure out what is going on with my ankle. The MRI showed nothing, but he cannot jump off this ankle and run down the basketball court without feeling pain. I just smiled. He asked, "What are you smiling about?" I said, "You're in luck. When you get back in town, look me up and come over to my clinic. I think I can get you back to playing basketball again."

He took my card, and then a few weeks later, he called me up and made a cross-town visit. I assessed his leg and ankle, and everything matched up with his ankle not tracking right. I told him what I wanted to do, explaining that I needed to release his ankle, then applied a natural injection called Prolotherapy to stabilize the joint.

"Anything that will get me playing again, just do it," he said.

I laid him back as I always do. I need him to be as relaxed as he can in order to perform the technique correctly. I then positioned the ankle in the proper alignment and watched his breathing. I released the ankle, holding it in a correct position, taking the shock out of it, and set the deeper bones of the ankle. I then followed up by injecting him with Prolotherapy. This natural glue holds everything in place. I put the proper ankle strapping on him and told him to follow up in a month.

I got a phone call the next morning; it was on a Saturday morning, my day off. When someone calls after hours or on the weekends, it means something needs to be addressed. He was telling me that he was in the gym, and that I am not going to believe that he slam-dunked the basketball with two hands. He did it by jumping off both feet. "This is the first time in over 6 months that I am able to do this. I am also running up and down the court without missing a step, and the training coach is asking me what I did," he exclaimed. I followed up with him a few more times to make sure the ankle was staying in its right place, and I have not seen him back since finishing that treatment with him.

I will share another more recent experience. I had a patient come into my office with severe foot pain. He was in college and was about to go to the Olympics in his event. He had beaten the highly favored swimmer who dominated the swimming with his gold medals. I will not go into details about his injury that resulted in surgery of the foot for personal and private reasons, but his competitive swimming days were over. He could not put the full force of his kick in the water because of the limited motion in his foot and ankle. He stumbled upon my clinic. I did my assessment and told him what I wanted to do. He was all for it. Even though his Olympic days are long gone, he just wanted to get back in the pool and swim without pain and with his explosive techniques like he used to do.

Not only was his ankle out of alignment, but also his midfoot. After releasing both, I did Prolotherapy to stabilize the various joints in his foot and ankle. He was so amazed by how his foot felt when he stood down, he was almost in tears. He said, "Had I known you when I was in rehab with my injury, maybe I could have gone to the Olympics." I followed up with him, and due to his injury, it was not just a one-and-done like most of my patients; it took a few more times to release the deeper adhesions and set it in the proper position. He is now back to swimming and walking without pain, and is a completely new person.

I have treated hundreds of patients over the years with Prolotherapy. I have repaired torn ligaments, Plantar fascia, and tendons, all with an MRI showing me the tear. I also followed up with another MRI on some of them to see if they were healed. A lot of the time, it is not necessary. Aside from these soft tissue injuries, I have also treated neuromas, a very painful forefoot condition. I have even sealed off damaged ganglion cysts in the foot without having to go into surgery and repair the injured area.

When I see a foot and ankle, I do not put a status on that foot, but only a treatment to get it better. Yes, that foot may be attached to a famous person, but in God's eyes, we are all important. I am eager to see and treat the person who wants to go back to work so they can provide for their family just as much as a professional athlete who wants to get back to playing their sport.

Thought Field Therapy TFT: Tapping Anxiety or Fear of a Needle Away

Thought Field Therapy (TFT) is a brief psychotherapy that combines tapping on specific meridian points with focusing on specific thoughts or feelings to alleviate emotional distress by balancing the body's energy system[5].

What I will say about Thought Field Therapy (TFT), it is a modality that is extremely practical and effective. I am now using this TFT to calm the anxiety of patients before getting a shot for an ingrown toenail procedure and many other things.

---

[5] GoodTherapy. (2018, March 8). *Thought Field Therapy (TFT): Benefits, techniques & how it works*. GoodTherapy. Retrieved October 22, 2025, from https://www.goodtherapy.org/learn-about-therapy/types/thought-field-therapy

I had a patient who was in an auto accident and had a brain injury. One of the triggers for her brain is any sign of a needle makes her scream and go into a place that she doesn't like to be. She told me all this after the fact when I gave her a shot to remove an ingrown toenail. She screamed bloody murder when I was doing everything to not cause any pain. It was just the event of the matter that set her off.

When she returned to have the other toenail removed, I showed her some tapping while I was injecting. She did not make a peep, and even though she noticed a difference with this simple technique, it is so powerful and helpful that I feel it can help all forms of emotional trauma.

This art of Jin Shin Jyutsu and Myopractics, along with TFT, has now been a gift to my practice, and it is helping transform the way I treat. Imagine a surgeon who was trained to cut is now advising his patient that there are other options other than surgery-that is me now. I have no regrets that I have shifted my focus to helping my patients.

Paired Organs Philosophy: To Treat the Lungs, You Treat the Large Intestine

I had a patient who was admitted to intensive care. He was having difficulty breathing, and so they needed to sedate him. Because I had helped this patient out over the years, I went down to the unit and asked to speak with the treating physician. I asked the doctor, "When was the last time the patient had a bowel movement?" He looked at his chart and said I don't see any time listed in his chart. I asked again, "How long has the patient been on the floor?" He responded by saying, "Several days." I advised that if they could get the patient to have a bowel movement, his breathing would get better. The doctor looked at me with a funny look. Still, he must have taken my advice and got the patient to have a bowel movement, because he sent me a text message thanking me for the information, and reported that the patient did what he asked.

His breathing started to improve, so he did not need to put him in the Intensive Care Unit.

On another occasion, a family member was in the hospital in Northern Utah at a teaching University. I told my family member I was coming up to see him, as his health was not in good shape; he had a severe lung infection. When I got there, the lung specialist was in the room, who was of oriental descent. He had been forewarned that I had some questions for him, which I did.

I asked him one simple question since it was a teaching hospital. I asked. "What is the correlation between the large intestine and the lung?" He looked at me and placed his right hand on his rib cage, and said that he worked from here up, with his hand running up to the throat. That was the end of the conversation. I learned a valuable lesson never to assume, as I felt he may be more inclined to understand the paired organ concept due to his ethnicity. The Paired Organ concept is found in my book *Healthy Dad Sick Dad* under the five-element chapter. I take you through this concept there in greater detail. Personally, if I have a lung issue, I am working on my intestines; it is that simple.

Infected Knee: "You Saved My Life"

I had one of my diabetic patients come into my office. He had just returned from his orthopedic surgeon, who had given him the green light that his total knee was good. When he came in for his diabetic checkup, I noticed something was wrong with his knee. He said, "I just saw the doctor yesterday and was told everything was ok." I insisted that he go to the emergency room immediately.

When he got there, it was confirmed that his knee was infected, and he was sent to the valley. I got a call from him, and he said they need to take the leg from above the knee due to the severity of the infection. "If they don't take the leg, then I will die. What would you do?"

I responded to him, "That depends. Do you feel like there are things you still want to accomplish?" He said, "Yes. I need to do a lot more."

I responded, "Then let them take your leg, and we will worry about the prosthetic and walking later."

They took his leg off above the knee, and he was fitted with a prosthetic leg. He was back to golfing and walking and still served as the dean at the local college. He is still very active. He thanks me every time he comes into my office and says, "There is a good doctor who saved my life."

In one of his last years as dean of the college, he had me be the commencement speaker at the graduation ceremony of his college students.

Walking in with a Cane and Forgetting It When He Left

I once had another patient come into my office; he had just been to his orthopedic doctor. He got an injection into his knee, and he walked into my clinic with pain. "I am flying out to Italy in a few days. I have this knee pain that will not go away. I had a shot, but that did not help, and the anti-inflammatories don't help either. Is there anything you can do?"

I said, "Did they ever look at your ankle?" He said, "No, it is my knee that hurts."

I laid him back, and with the testing that I did, I knew his ankle was not tracking right. I told him what I was going to do and got the release I was looking for. When he stood up and began to walk, he was so excited that there was no pain in his knee. As he was heading out the door, he realized he had left his cane in my room. He came back for it and gave me a big hug and thanked me.

Are We Eating Poisons and Don't Know It?

A lady came into my office. She told me, "You are the 7th doctor, and nobody has figured out the pain in my feet." I asked her specific questions, thinking the pain was only in the legs and feet. She corrected me that it was in her entire body. I asked her, "Do you drink any diet soda?" She admitted to drinking two six packs a day.

"I want you to do something," I advised, "I want you to go home, open the remaining diet drink you have, and dump it down the drain. Don't drink another diet soda for the next two weeks. You're going to have a headache at first, but it will improve." I could see in her face that she wasn't convinced and might be thinking of looking for an 8th doctor. Still, she agreed and came back two weeks later. I took a second look at her when she came in; she was completely pain-free. The main ingredient in diet soda is Aspartame, which is a neurotoxin. Sometimes you must look outside the box to see what is in the box. In her case, it was what was in her soda.

Fungus Among Us

There are other conditions that I deal with that I use a more holistic approach to healing. Let's take, for instance, fungal toenails. When I see a fungal toenail, the first thing that I think of is the immune system. We all have some degree of bacteria, fungi, and viruses in our bodies. When it breaks through the threshold, then symptoms are seen. Fungus is no different, in my opinion. It starts with an injury, and if the immune system is depleted, the person will show fungus. A person with a strong immune system will not see the fungus arise. My protocol for fungal toenails is soaking in baking soda and warm water. I found this out by reading a book about twelve years ago entitled *Cancer is a Fungus* by Dr. T. Simoncini, who said all cancers are fungal-related. So, I started soaking in baking soda, and my patient started to get better. I then changed their diet, establishing probiotics in the system to offset the bad system. Once the person can get off the sugars, GMO foods, and preservatives, they are on the road to a stronger immune system. Maybe one day there will be more people talking about fungal toenails and looking at the immune system to help, as I have done for the past 20 years.

I am often asked what my diet is. My response is that I eat to maintain my body temperature, which is the best way to protect my immune system. So, one day I could be a complete vegan, but the next day I will be eating a nice salmon or chicken.

Autism: This Is the First Time My Boy Spoke

I had a young child come into my office who had autism. His mom wanted him to be fitted for orthotics, but the child could not talk. His mom said he had not yet learned to talk in class at school. Even though she intended to get orthotics for his child, I asked her if she would be willing to try a diet that would help her child. I showed her the immune diet and told her specific things to avoid and eat. Then I cast her son for the custom-made orthotics and told her we would call when they come in. It was about three but closer to four weeks when they came back in. "You're not going to believe this," she exclaimed, "Ever since you showed us this diet, my son has been speaking and talking in school." This child even said hi to me when he was going into the exam room to get his custom-made orthotics.

Neuromas: You have Neuropathy; Let's Put You on This Medication

I see these every day, but I have only taken one out in my entire private practice career. These are those pesky painful balls of the feet presentations. A lot of times, people will come to me because they were told they have neuropathy and placed on medication. Then, years later, they still have this pain. I once had a patient who was placed on medication for ten years for this foot pain. After listening to me give a lecture, he decided to schedule an appointment with me. I assessed that his diagnosis was a Neuroma and not neuropathy, and gave a simple injection, then worked the tissue in a specific way. I asked him to come back in two weeks. He was pain-free and off his medication. I have not seen him back, and that was over fifteen years ago.

Bunions: Your Upper Opposite Shoulder Is Causing Your Problem

These deformities are unique. I was always told that bunions are genetic; somebody in the family had them. My response is that someone in your family is just as stressed as you are. I notice that bunions are either an injury to the opposite upper back and neck area, or it is an emotional trauma (spending too much time on future worries). Yes, when I look at your feet, I can see where else in your body that is holding the stresses of life.

One of the surgeries in Podiatry that really never made sense to me was that of bunions. There are over a hundred ways to fix one, but there really is no talk of correcting it without surgery. They mention how to reduce them and stop them from growing through custom-made orthotics, and you will see some YouTube episodes trying to show you how to reduce the bump. Still, they have never shown you the source of why you got your bunion in the first place. It has always been my mission to fix bunions without surgery. Once I started learning about Myopractics, I found that my techniques work, as the hundreds of patients that I have seen have not had to go into surgery, and the bunion doesn't hurt anymore.

Shortly after my divorce, my right bunion went south, and it was painful. I did not want surgery, so I set out to find a cure other than surgery. I implemented a three-stretching technique along with relaxing the upper body. Then the one thing that takes the pain out of the joint is the subtle manipulation, just like the ankle. It is also very effective to have the upper body and mid back worked on through manipulation to truly reduce a bunion back into place.

Today, you could not even tell that I have a bunion in my foot. Bunions are always associated with opposite shoulder pain. If you have a right-sided bunion, then something is going on with your left shoulder, neck, and mid-upper back. It can either be an emotional injury or a physical injury; most of the ones I see come from too much thinking or worrying about everything. When you are stressed, your body wants to be in balance, so subtly your toes grip more and cause more contraction and misalignment, and then one day you see these bumps on your great toe.

I remember one day I had six patients who wanted bunion surgery because of the pain; all 6 of them were pain-free when they left the office. One went on to have surgery because they wanted the bump gone, even though they were pain-free.

I had a 16-year-old girl come into my office with an ingrown toenail, but I noticed she had a bunion. I told her that if you did these stretching exercises, the bunion would be reduced. I also showed her what to do for the upper back. When she came back two weeks later, I looked at her foot and then had to look at the notes to see which foot the bunion was on because there was no sign of a bunion in either foot.

If I can get a bunion in the beginning stages, I feel they will never need to go on to have surgery. If you are reading this and you have a bunion, relax your opposite shoulder and neck, stay away from the future talk of fears, worries of life, stretch the calf muscle daily, and do the three forms of stretching in the feet.

Outer Leg Pains: I Have Been Having This Unexplained Pain for Years

I see this almost every day; a patient will come in with a condition called tarsal tunnel syndrome. It is the same thing in the wrist called carpal tunnel syndrome. They will also express to me this pain that is on the outer leg and up into the outer thigh of the upper leg. It is most always biomechanical. It is the shoes they are wearing or not wearing, and the surface they are standing on. When I can get a release in the foot and or ankle, it usually takes away the pressure and pain.

Some need to go on and have Prolotherapy, some need to have an injection to calm down the nerve, like in the case of tarsal tunnel syndrome. I get great joy out of helping people with these conditions. They are usually frustrated patients who have been to several other doctors but are still in pain. They have spent thousands of dollars on these over-the-counter inserts, but what I have learned is that when people are in pain, they will go to great lengths to find relief.

This type of conditions is the main thing I see in my practice. I don't know how and why these types of conditions show up in my office, but I don't ask why or how; I just treat them. I feel somehow, they are guided to my office. If you have unexplained pain going up your outer leg, could it be as simple as releasing a few joints in the foot, and all your pain is gone? I can't tell you the countless patients who have come into my office with this pain, and after months and years of pain, they are pain-free.

Why I Wear Two Colored Pairs of Shoes in the Clinic

COVID changed the world, and a lot did not make sense to me from the beginning. I know the importance of wearing a mask in surgery, but why do you have to wear one on the beach or outside, and if they were so important, why were the homeless people not dying left and right?

One way I combated being asked why I don't wear a mask in the clinic is by wearing two pairs of colored shoes. I figured people are so used to looking down at their phones that they would obviously see my two different colored pairs of shoes. By the time they realized I did not have a mask on and could say something to me,

I was gone. I still wear those two-colored pairs of shoes today. Today I just say, you can't take life seriously, or it will kill you!

When I was prohibited from doing surgery because I did not take the shot that was required for all medical personnel, I had to figure out more things in the clinic. I learned how to handle way more things that had to be done in the clinic, where some of the cases I would have taken to the operating room—fractures, loose bodies in the joints, and foreign bodies, to name a few. I feel the era of COVID strengthened my clinical skills; I listened more to the patient. I incorporated more of the myofascial release, Jin Shin Jyutsu, and TFT.

I spent my entire life in college and medical school preparing to be a surgeon. I still look at myself as a surgeon, but now I do surgery only when it is necessary, and my clinical skills don't work, which sometimes is the case. I am indebted to those who trained me and showed me the art of surgery, but I am also very thankful to those who have taught me the alternative ways of helping people. I feel I have the best of both worlds. Taking on this new way of treating patients has been a lonely road; I find that it is difficult to talk with my colleagues. But I am ok traveling on this road because of the success in helping so many people who come into my office. Both worlds have blessed me—Western medicine, which showed the importance of surgery, and Eastern medicine, which has shown me how to help people who are looking at other options other than surgery to fix their health complaints.

At some points in life, we are asked to climb some impossible mountain peaks. When we are at our lowest, it is as if we are in the valley looking up to the peak we are to climb, and we end up talking ourselves out of the journey. There is a famous saying that says, "I did not say it would be easy, but it would be worth it."

My lowest time in life came when my kids stopped communicating with me. I had a choice to stay in the valley or climb out of it and see the potential that was mine to claim. It was one of the most difficult journeys, a journey full of lumps and bumps, but each milestone showed me what was possible. They say Mount Everest is the tallest peak–I disagree. The person who stands on the peak at that moment in time becomes the tallest peak on earth. I feel I have climbed Mount Everest, and I am standing on top of it, looking over the vastness of knowledge and wisdom that is there for our taking. I hope to continue to ask the questions that create the conversation that leads to growth and opportunities.

Reflection

What I've learned at the bedside, on the sidelines, and in the quiet of the clinic is this: change begins with one honest breath and one brave choice–and you can make both today. Listen to your body's whispers before they become shouts. Look past the obvious pain to the real source. Release what is tight–joints, habits, grudges. Stabilize what matters–your boundaries, routines, and faith. Nourish what makes you stronger–whole foods, hopeful thoughts, and the people who lift you. Integrate what you learn–small, steady practices that compound into powerful results.

When life hands you a mountain, don't argue with the climb: smile, question kindly, pray boldly, and take the next right step. You don't need perfect conditions to rise; you need persistence, humility, and a willingness to see symptoms as signposts, not life sentences. Let courage–not convention–set your pace. Lighten up (a little humor goes a long way), honor your whole self, and choose progress over drama. Healing and growth are not events–they are daily rhythms of attention and intention.

Start where you are, use what you have, and move forward with grace. One thoughtful, compassionate step at a time, you'll look up and realize: you are standing on your own summit.

CHAPTER 14

I Didn't Say It Would Be Easy, but It Was Worth It

Yea, I know that I am Nothing as to my strength I am weak; therefore, I will not boast of myself, but I will boast of my God for in his strength, I can do All things.

— Ammon

Show Them. What a perfect title– "**Show Them.**"

My entire life has been a life of showing my true potential. I just used their negative projections and words to achieve success. All somebody had to do was tell me I couldn't, and I just did the opposite. I just **Show Them**!

From a child holding a razor blade to open up a cow heart in the 6th grade, to graduating to a pocket knife enabling me to castrate pigs on the farm, to holding a scalpel with a surgical blade and exploring the human body like Leonardo da Vinci did when he studied anatomy to paint the human body. To gowning up in a sterile setting and opening the skin of a consented patient and fixing what needed to be fixed. All these chapters have caused me to pause and reflect on the journey that took me through each phase and how blessed I was to participate in each experience.

Was it worth it to create my own asthma attacks as I set out to find a cure for asthma? Yes, it was, and I would do it again.

Was it worth it to stand in front of the counselor's desk and listen to the three-sentence recommendations on what he thought I should do with my life? Yes, it was because it allowed my true self to shine, the self that held all the keys to unlocking my true potential to accomplish whatever I set out to accomplish: my mind's imagination.

Was it worth it knowing I never graduated with a bachelor's degree but made it into medical school? As embarrassing as it was for me to stand among the other classmates with degrees from prestigious Universities, it did not matter when we all walked across the stage to receive our Doctorate Degree in Podiatric Medicine. Yes, D stands for doctor.

Was it worth it sleeping on a laundry room floor and at a bus stop while trying to find a place to live in my first semester in school? Yes, it was because when you think nobody cares about you, there is always the one who watches your every step and will direct you to those few individuals who have a caring heart and understand the purpose of life. Life is not a competition with each other but a stretched-out hand that helps lift up those around them.

Was it worth failing the National Board Part I four times before I finally passed on my last attempt? Yes, for it taught me one of life's great lessons that persistence and perseverance in your conviction is your bucket of gold at the end of the rainbow.

Was it worth it to take the journey to the other side and go through the pains of death to want to live so I could fulfill a promise? There is no question about this one. My answer is yes, to have a second chance in life and share it with those who are ready to pass on, or to hug a person who has lost a loved one and help them understand that the spirit continues to live on.

It is only the body that rests. I am so thankful for this gift and to be given a second chance in life, and for helping save that man's life in South Dakota; I am sure he has since passed on by now. Still, it was at his time that God chose to take him back, and not a medical reason that takes so many of us sooner than our expiration date. Yes, I miss both of my parents who have passed on. I was so grateful to help my father with his stepping into the other side, and five weeks later, I watched my mother's beautiful smile join him.

Was it worth it, missing my boy's 1st birthday so I could go and save a ten-year-old life on a remote island in the South Pacific and fulfill an eleven-year-old promise? Yes, it was. Sometimes in life, we do things that others don't understand. Still, with time, maybe they will see that true service is the meaning of life and promises are recorded in the heavens to create miracles when they are fulfilled.

Was it worth it to experience a painful divorce? This time in my life, when I felt I was pushed beyond what I was able to handle, it made me stop and think a bit. I remember very clearly that day I wanted to end it because I thought I had lost everything. But here is my answer—the answer is very simple! Hell, yes, it was worth it. Because I defeated hell as I walked through it, and now each day is a gift from heaven. Xanthi has shown me what love is. I am so thankful to her for buying my easel to start painting and encouraging me to write and share my experiences with others. If you stop and think about it, the children we claim that are ours, they are only on lease; they belong to God, they are his children. If Jesus was raised by a stepfather, then why should it be any different for me, and I greater than him? No.

Was it worth it to become a surgeon, but now to offer other options other than surgery? Yes, but don't get me wrong, I love being in the operative room. There is no other humbling experience than that of holding a scalpel in your hand, opening the skin of a human being, exploring and fixing a place that no one has ever touched, and then trying to put it back together as good as the original creator. It is truly breathtaking.

I see beauty each day when I open my eyes, and I have a spirit of gratitude when those same eyes are closed at night, as I venture off into a new dream. God said it would not be easy, but it would be worth it. Let's look at our own experiences as our life teacher. We will understand that challenges, disappointment, and failures are only part of the journey. Use them to your advantage, and springboard them to your goals and desires. I am so grateful to my math teacher in college, who said, "When you're faced with a challenge, just look at it as another way to succeed."

The key to life is to think "balanced." When you feel Angry or Frustrated, feel its opposite—Compassion and Thanksgiving. When you feel Guilty or Shame, think Forgive and Kindness. When you feel Worried or Fear, think Faith and Gratitude. If you can be aware of your emotions, the words you say to others, and, even more importantly, to yourself, you will become the binding force of a promise etched in the heavens that will not allow you to fail.

Remember, you literally are a piece of God. You have his spiritual DNA inside of you, and you can be, do, and have anything you set your mind to. Just smile and enjoy the journey.

Sometimes the only person that you can rely on is God; he is always there to help show you the way. When I was going through my darkest days, I would question why God was allowing me to go through this. Some days, I even cursed and questioned his existence, even with all my little miracles that I have had in my life. What I can tell you, we need to take the first step towards him before he intervenes.

Maybe that is why those days were so dark, because I did not take the first step towards him. Maybe my ego got in the way, and I just used my willpower to get through those dark days. How easier would it have been to fall to my knees and say a silent prayer and just listen? I hope by sharing my stories, I can save you the headache of future events. Just go to the source, and he will help you in your journey.

My only advice is that whatever you're going through at this time, let go and let God. We obtain titles in life, such as a doctor, surgeon, artist, husband, or father; in the end, we are really No Thing when we do it alone. But we are All Things when we allow God to be a partner in our journey. Try not to go at it alone because it is a very lonely road. Trust me, I have been there.

The Million Mile Journey

I may not have walked a million miles myself, but if you take all the stories of my patients over the course of my 26 years in private practice, it is well over a million miles walked; from the patient who drove General Patton in WWII, to the patient who landed on Normandy beach to defeat the Germans, to the patients who pitched in the World Series against the Yankees and against all the legendary players like Joe DiMaggio, Hank Arron and Jackie Robinson, and to the feet that planted firmly in the sod of Super Bowl II.

To the patient who danced in some of the largest stages in Europe, to the hiker who just completed the Continental hikes, and to the patient who sent me a photo from the Great Wall of China with her fracture foot in a boot.

To the monk in Indonesia who helps his followers find happiness in life, and to the professional basketball player who was told he would never play again, but after one treatment, he walked on to the basketball court and slammed dunked a basketball pain-free.

To the patients who put on their dress shoes and went to work in the corporate offices, to the patient who used his feet to swim with some of the greats, to the patient who put his life at risk to save his two children as they crossed the border, and to the first responders who truly save lives each day.

To the tens of thousands of feet that I have treated over the years, thank you for allowing me to hear your foot stories of disappointments, challenges, and even near-death experiences, such as myself.

My Promise to You

When life tells you "you can't," pause, look inward, and listen for the desire God placed in you–then use every doubt as fuel to **Show Them** (and yourself) what you're truly capable of. Meet setbacks with persistence, pain with purpose, and fear with faith, because while the path won't be easy, it will be worth it.

Choose balance by replacing anger with compassion, worry with gratitude, and shame with forgiveness; prepare as if the breakthrough is already on its way, keep your promises, and serve others along your million-mile journey.

Let your titles be tools, not your identity, and partner with God so "no thing" becomes all things. Each day, INJOY—find your joy within and express it through thankfulness—then lift your head, steady your heart, and step forward with courage; this is your time to rise, to persist, to love, to keep walking, and to **SHOW THEM** your God-given potential—because yes, it's worth it.

A Journey of Redemption and Growth

My life has been a tapestry woven with trials and triumphs, each thread representing a moment that has shaped my character and my faith. Through every challenge I faced, I have come to understand the profound influence of God and Jesus Christ in my journey.

From my early years, I encountered obstacles that seemed insurmountable. I struggled with self-doubt, especially during my school years, when my guidance counselor told me that I would never make it to college. Those words could have defined my future, but instead, they ignited a fire within me. I remember praying for strength and guidance during those difficult times, seeking assurance that there was a greater purpose for my life.

When I embarked on my mission, I was far away from family and friends, relying solely on my faith. It was during those two years of service that I truly learned the value of prayer and connection with God. I witnessed countless miracles—whether it was helping a family find their way through their struggles or being a source of comfort to those in need. Each experience reinforced my belief that God has a plan for each of us, and through Him, we can find purpose and joy.

The Power of Prayer

Every day, I begin and end on my knees, offering thanks and seeking guidance. I remember one particular moment when I faced a life-threatening situation; I felt the presence of God surrounding me. I prayed fervently for my life, and in that moment, I felt an overwhelming peace wash over me. It was a reminder that I was not alone, that my life has meaning beyond my understanding.

As I transitioned back to civilian life and pursued my education, I faced numerous hurdles, including academic failures and personal setbacks. Yet, through each trial, I turned to Christ, who provided me with strength and resilience. I learned that failure is not the end; it is merely a stepping stone toward success. With every setback, I found the determination to rise again, fueled by the belief that my efforts were not in vain.

Embracing My True Potential

Through my studies and professional journey, I have felt God's hand guiding me. I have been blessed to serve those in need, and each patient I encounter reminds me of the divine purpose in my calling. My heart swells with gratitude for the opportunity to care for others, knowing that I am fulfilling a mission that extends beyond myself.

Jesus taught us to love one another, and in that love, I have found healing and fulfillment. I have learned that true joy comes not from material success or accolades but from serving others and building meaningful relationships. I strive to embody this love in every aspect of my life, whether in my personal interactions or my professional pursuits.

A Life Transformed

Today, I stand as a testament to the transformative power of faith. The challenges I have faced have equipped me with empathy, resilience, and a deep understanding of the human experience. I am no longer defined by my past failures but rather by the growth that has come from them. I have learned to see every obstacle as an opportunity for growth, and every setback as a chance to lean on my faith.

To anyone reading this, I encourage you to embrace your journey and seek a deeper connection with God and Jesus Christ. Your heart can be filled with hope and purpose, and your life can be transformed in ways you never imagined. Trust in His plan, and know that with faith, all things are possible.

The adventure of life is just beginning, and I am excited to see where this path of faith leads. Together, we can navigate our challenges, celebrate our victories, and inspire one another to reach our true potential. Let us walk forward with courage, guided by the light of faith in our hearts.

Stop Managing Pain. Start Reversing Conditions. Foot and Ankle Health, Re-imagined.

Experience True Healing. Get a Customized Plan That Addresses Your Body's Whole Health.

Dr. Glen N. Robison, DPM, of AZ Foot and Ankle, offers an unparalleled, 25-year proven approach that views foot and ankle issues not just as local problems, but as reflections of overall health. His mission is to heal naturally, combining advanced podiatric medicine with holistic therapies to provide you with a lasting solution.

The Robison Difference: Comprehensive, Customized, and Cost-Effective Care

Dr. Robison's commitment to personalized care is delivered through a unique set of integrated skills:

Holistic Expertise: As a highly skilled Podiatric Specialist Physician/Surgeon and a seasoned practitioner of Jin Shin Jyutsu and Myopractic, Dr. Robison performs a deep, full-body evaluation. This allows him to restore energy flow, correct alignment, and find the root cause of your condition.

Targeted Natural Solutions: Get customized success with stubborn conditions:

Bunion Reversal: Explore non-surgical protocols to correct and reverse bunions.

Neuropathy Relief: Achieve remarkable success in treating neuropathy at a fraction of the cost of traditional methods.

The Diet Connection: Address systemic causes of foot and ankle issues with personalized, preventative diet management plans designed to minimize symptoms of:

- Diabetes Diet
- Fungus Diet
- Gout Diet
- Immune Diet

Surgical Mastery (If Needed): If conservative, natural healing is not enough, you are in the hands of a highly skilled Podiatric Surgeon with over two decades of experience, ensuring the absolute highest standard of care and the best surgical outcomes.

You don't have to live with pain or accept the most extreme treatment first. Choose a doctor who treats you holistically and prioritizes natural healing.

Take the Next Step: Choose Natural Healing. Choose Dr. Robison.

Call now to schedule your comprehensive evaluation and start your journey toward complete, lasting foot and ankle health.

Practice AZ Foot and Ankle
Location 6242 E Arbor Ave #116, Mesa, AZ 85206
Phone (480) 984-3338
Website DrGlenRobison.com

Dedication

To my mom, who **Showed** me the beauty that thoughts in our mind will take you places you only dream and read about. I am so thankful to her for never doubting me; she knew I could do it.

To Corona, my Christ-like brother who **Showed** me that promises are so powerful to affect the entire universe.

To Xanthi, my wife, who **Shows** me every day that angels do exist.

To the thousands of patients who allowed me to be a part of their foot journey that caused them to come into my office. Thank you for taking me on this million-mile journey.

To my Elder brother, Jesus Christ, who **Showed** me the way, the truth, and the light, I look forward to personally telling you Thank You one day.

To my father above, Thank You for answering my prayers each time I reached out to you for help. I can't wait to come back home, but only on your timetable.

Priceless gift from a patient in Tonga.

Xanthi, Glen, O and Tsar

About the Author

Dr. Glen N. Robison is a diplomate of the American Board of Multiple Specialties in Podiatry and board-certified in primary care in podiatric medicine with over twenty-six years of clinical and surgical experience.

A certified Jin Shin Jyutsu practitioner, TFT Voice Technology practitioner/certified TFT diagnostic trainer, and certified in Myopractor, Dr. Robison uses all three of these expertise areas to address deep restrictions in the body that contribute to pain and ailments and to help with releasing deep-seated emotional blockages that affect one's health.

He currently specializes in Prolotherapy to treat ankle instability, torn ligaments, tendons, and bunions without surgery.

He is the Amazon bestseller author of *Healthy Dad, Sick Dad: What Good Is Your Wealth If You Don't Have Your Health?* and Co-author of the USA Today bestseller *Luminary Leadership: How Top Entrepreneurs Lead in Business and in Life* and USA National Bestseller *Success DNA: Mastering Resistance in Leadership and Life.*

Dr. Robison has contributed to hands across the world with a medical mission to the Kingdom of Tonga in 2000.

Outside his podiatric medical practice, he enjoys realism oil painting and playing with his two bundles of joy, Tsar and O. He currently resides in Arizona with his beautiful wife, Xanthi.

Learn more about what I do: www.drglenrobison.com